Above & Below

Christ church
Christiana Hundred,
Wilmington, Delaware

St. Barnabas,
Wilmington, Delaware

St. Martha's,
Bethany Beach, Delaware

Above & Below

Reflections on the Spiritual Journey

David Beresford

Brookscraft Publishing

Above & Below

Reflections on the Spiritual Journey

.

Published 2026 by:
Brookscraft Publishing.
Buffalo, New York 14203
info@brookscraftpublishing.com
www.brookscraftpublishing.com

First Published in 2021 by Cedar Tree Books.

ISBN: 978-1-969682-33-9 EBOOK
ISBN: 978-1-969682-34-6 PAPERBACK
ISBN: 978-1-969682-35-3 HARDCOVER

Title: Above & Below, Reflections on the Spiritual Journey
Author: David Beresford
Editor: Nick Cerchio
Book Design: Bob Schwartz
Cover image: Urtė Milda Širvinskaitė/shutterstock.com

Copyright: © 2021 David Beresford

Unless otherwise noted, Scripture quotations are from:
The New Revised Standard Version Bible
©1989 National Council of the Churches of Christ in the United States of America. Used with permission.

Printed and bound in the United States of America

— Dedication —

To my brothers and sisters at
St. Martha's, Bethany Beach, St. Barnabas, Wilmington,
and Christ Church Christiana Hundred, Wilmington.

I was a stranger and you welcomed me.
(Matthew 25:35)

— Preface —

The meditations in this book were written for two congregations in the Diocese of Delaware: St. Barnabas, Wilmington, where I served as interim Rector between May 2019 and July 2020, and St. Martha's, Bethany Beach, where I served in the same capacity from August 2020 to July 2021.

They are pastoral letters to the members of the church, written before and during the onset of the coronavirus SARS-CoV-2, a.k.a. Covid-19. For two separate periods in 2020 and 2021, the doors of the church were closed to public worship. The question foremost in my mind at that time was: "how are we still the church when we cannot assemble?" The meditations, posted on a Friday (St. Barnabas) or Saturday (St. Martha's), were intended to keep members thinking about their faith, and to inform, entertain and help them stay connected to the church.

Writing a weekly letter, along with a sermon, was a demanding discipline. Some weeks I would know exactly what to say; at other times, I would pace the floor trying to think of a suitable topic. As much as possible I wanted to draw upon real life experiences, past and present, and offer a faith-based focus.

The weekly column at St. Barnabas came under the heading of "Life in Christ," which was intended to reflect an integrated and Christ- centered view of life. At St. Martha's, the column was called "Saturday Inspiration," a title already established when I arrived. When the "inspirations" were later posted on the website, it came under the heading of "Grains of Sand" (from Psalm 139:18). Each article was like a grain of sand on the beach; in the grand scheme of things, of little consequence, but enjoyable for me to write and I hope for the members to read.

In preparing this collection, I have noticed in the original letters some shortcomings in style and theological clarity—a result, no doubt, of writing to a weekly deadline. I have therefore taken this opportunity to revise and occasionally expand some of them. Only one—Learning to Forgive—was completely re-written.

Here then, all in one place, is a selection of those weekly "inspirations." Each can be read as a daily meditation, which would cover the period of one month. There is advice on prayer, forgiveness, and on seeing God in our midst. There are meditations on art and music. There is even a meditation about my cat, who once helped me to write a sermon.

I am continually inspired by the world God has created, and I hope you will take inspiration and pleasure from reading these reflections.

David Beresford

September 2021

— Foreword —

Some years ago, when I was a parish priest, a parishioner phoned me and asked anxiously, "Can we meet today? I really need your help." She paused, and I could hear the stress in her voice: "I don't feel God anymore. Where is God?" She explained that she had been a Christian all her life and a regular churchgoer for years, but now in her late thirties she was losing sleep that the comfort and security she had always known was now (forever?) beyond her reach. Was God angry? Had she made a mistake? "What is wrong?" she repeated. "Can I find God again?"

In a thousand different ways, this plea exemplifies the core of a priest's call: to help people to know and find God, whether for the first time or the second or sixtieth. This is part of the fabric of priesthood. Whether leading worship or teaching classes or praying with the sick or blessing the dying, a priest hopes to be a lens that helps others not only see the power of God in Christ Jesus but, even more, to see God's abundant love as sharply and clearly as possible.

And this is exactly what Fr. David has done throughout this wonderful collection of essays and reflections. Time and again, David's letters helps us his readers—originally his parishioners, the people looking directly to him for wisdom and guidance—focus anew on the presence of God around them. Whether through a quiet walk in the woods or a day trip with his wife or the poetry of e e cummings, David captures the deep truth that God remains ever-present to us in everyday life. Will we stop long enough to look for it? Under David's guidance, we pause again to look and feel, to taste and see. God is good, God is love, and God is here.

The Rt. Rev. Kevin S. Brown
Bishop of the Episcopal Church in Delaware

— Table of Contents —

— Acknowledgements —

My loving companion throughout the many changes and challenges of the past three years has been my wife, Ruth. We shared many of the adventures described within, and she was often the first person to read these reflections. I have relied upon her judgement and constructive criticism when revising them.

I would like to thank my publisher, Nick Cerchio, for his expertise, encouragement, and guidance. He has made the journey as smooth as possible for this novice writer. I am also grateful to the designer Bob Schwartz, for creating the book's distinctive layout and design.

Finally I want to express my gratitude to the original readers of the weekly "inspirations," who responded so positively to them. Because of their encouragement, these spiritual essays are now being published.

Above & Below

The sun also ariseth, and the sun goeth down, and hasteth to his place where he arose.

The wind goeth toward the south, and turneth about unto the north; it whirleth about continually, and the wind returneth again according to his circuits.

All the rivers run into the sea; yet the sea is not full; unto the place from whence the rivers come, thither they return again.

—Ecclesiastes 1:5–7 (KJV)

St. Barnabas

Wilmington

Woodstock

August 22, 2019

L ast week was the 50th anniversary of the music festival at Woodstock. There have been a number of articles looking back at that event, and on Amazon Prime a new documentary tells the story from the perspective of the organizers and those who attended. I saw the original movie when it first came out, albeit one with cuts for nudity and bad language, in a school party, presumably because our teachers thought it would be educational.

It was in the cinema, and not in church, that I had my first religious experience. It came at the end of the movie, when Jimi Hendrix was playing the Star Spangled Banner. Sitting close to the screen, and with the speakers at full volume, I was transfixed by what I was seeing and hearing: this was music, not from another planet, but from another universe.

Woodstock. It's all about the music, right? That's why there was a festival in the first place, but the three days of Peace and Music quickly mythologized into something else. We now refer to the "Woodstock Generation," which is really a kind of shorthand for the social changes taking place at the time, against the background of the Vietnam War. It was a time before cellphones, when you could be three days away from your parents and have no contact with them. (And do whatever you wanted).

What a lot of people did was drugs. Pot, or even worse, Gallo Californian wine, (see the new documentary). LSD had its heyday around this time too, although not everyone was a believer: John Fogerty and Pete

Townshend, who played at the festival, hated the influence of drugs. Drugs formed part of the alternative lifestyle that became the hippie culture, which later included living in communes and rejecting the prevailing "rat race" culture. Hippies as a group didn't last long. The punks who came only eight years later despised them—"never trust a hippie" snarled John Lydon.

What happened to the hippies? Most became respectable, went to college, or became stockbrokers like Jerry Rubin. Two years ago I attended a concert by one of my musical heroes, Eric Burdon. Halfway through the second song he removed his jacket and on the back of his t-shirt were the words "I used to be a hippie." Like Woodstock, hippies exist today as a memory of a different time, when people were more idealistic and it was possible for people in close proximity to get along peacefully for three days.

Is the importance placed on Woodstock as a cultural event overblown? Everyone knows the movie, but I also remember another, now forgotten, festival movie made a year later, called "We Have Come for Your Daughters". That memorably captures scenes of hippies arguing and squabbling like, well, normal folk. Perhaps the hippies weren't so different after all. But nobody knows that movie now, perhaps because it sheds a different light on what was happening at the time.

The most famous song about Woodstock was actually written by someone who wasn't there: Joni Mitchell wrote "Woodstock," which carries the line "We've got to get ourselves back to the garden." She is expressing a yearning for an age of innocence, when Adam and Eve lived without shame in the garden of Eden. The song was a further act of mythologizing. But what about the reality?

I wasn't at Woodstock, but I went to a three day music festival in the late 1970s. I was with a group of friends, and we put up a tent and drank beer and enjoyed the village atmosphere. Unlike Woodstock, it never rained, so we didn't have to put up with mud and with everything being soaked. The music was great. The only down side was that the people in the tent next to us had their stuff stolen.

At Woodstock they ran out of food, but ladies of the local Jewish community center prepared 30,000 sandwiches that were handed out by local nuns. The promoters lost money, as did Max Yasgur, the farmer who allowed his land to be the site for the festival. He was later sued by neighbors over damage caused by the large number of people who attended. LSD laced with rat poison made many festival goers ill. Many festival goers left before the end, especially after the rain turned everything to mud. Three of the best creative lights who played at the festival—Jimi Hendrix, Janis Joplin and Alan "Blind Owl" Wilson—died the following year.

Strip away the mythologizing and the legacy of Woodstock is primarily a musical one. In fact, the popularity of the counter-cultural movement, if we can still call it that, rested on the quality of the music, most of which still sounds good today, despite (or perhaps because of) the primitive recording technology of the time. This year a 38 CD box set of the festival, limited to 1,969 copies and selling for $800, sold out within a week.

Woodstock veteran David Crosby recently recorded a new version of the song "Woodstock." I thought to myself, surely the last thing the world needs is another step into the past. Why don't these old hippies let it go? Then I heard the song and admired its fragile beauty and the poignancy of the words and I was again transfixed. It was the music, I recall, which drew me in the first time. Despite the cynicism of years, a part of me rejoices that I can still respond in an idealistic way to a simple message of peace and love.

Father David

Paul in the Middle

September 5, 2019

I n the New Testament, in between the gospels and Revelation, are letters written by the apostles who are explaining the Christian faith for the benefit of new converts. They are attempting to answer questions such as, "What does it mean to be a Christian?" and "Who is Jesus Christ?" The letters open to us the mind of the early Christian, formed by Judaism, but also influenced and shaped by Greco- Roman culture. Along with theological discussions on the nature of God, truth and reality, there is advice on how to live as Christians: what constitutes proper Christian behavior in society?

While many of the letters are long and often provide Christian teachers with a wealth of educational material—enough to last several weeks—a handful of the letters are short and can be read in less than five minutes. One of these is the Letter to Philemon, written by the apostle Paul around the year AD 60. The letter reveals something important about human relationships in the early Christian age: regardless of differences in social status, Christians were expected to think of one another as brothers and sisters in Christ.

The Letter to Philemon (pronounced Fye-lee´-mon) is a personal letter. One might wonder why it was included at all, since there is none of the sermonizing or theology you find in his other letters, such as the letter to the Romans, or in the letters to the fledgling church at Corinth. Philemon was a well-off convert to Christianity, whose house had become a meeting place for worshipping Christians. Like all personal letters, it tells us something about the relationship between the two parties. Paul obviously thinks highly of Philemon, and praises him for sharing the faith with others, especially, as Paul puts it, in "refreshing the saints," a phrase which could mean financial support. The word "saints" here simply means believers.

It's a letter which is as well known for what it doesn't say as for what it does say. Unfortunately, we don't have a copy of Philemon's reply, if he ever wrote one. And because it describes persons and events without being fully explicit about them, there is a temptation for us, when we read the letter, to make various assumptions about them. However, some speculation may help to unlock one or two of the letter's mysteries.

Paul writes from prison—he doesn't say where. Perhaps Rome, but more likely Asia Minor, possibly Colossae or Ephesus. While in prison Paul meets a young man called Onesimus, who happens to be Philemon's slave, and Paul is writing to Philemon about him. We don't know how or why Onesimus met Paul. This has generated a great deal of speculation from scholars. Was Onesimus in prison with Paul? That's unlikely, since slaves were imprisoned in separate areas to Roman citizens, of whom Paul was one. Was Onesimus on the run from Philemon? Perhaps, but why? Had he stolen money? What wrong had he done to Philemon? We don't know. All we know is that in the letter Paul offers to repay Philemon any debt, monetary or otherwise, that Onesimus owes Philemon.

It is probable that Onesimus seeks Paul out in the first place. It may be to ask Paul the favor of interceding on his behalf with his master. There are other examples of non-Christian letters of the time which do this. Perhaps Onesimus was not much good as a slave—incompetent, unhappy, bungling—and if bought in the market place, for Philemon a bad investment. Whatever the reason, Onesimus has probably heard Paul spoken of highly at his master's house and decides to seek him out. As it turns out, he gets more than he bargains for, since when he and Paul meet, Paul converts Onesimus to the Christian faith, probably baptizing him in prison.

The two forge a strong spiritual friendship and, instead of returning immediately to his master, Onesimus becomes one of Paul's helpers during Paul's incarceration. In Paul's eyes, Onesimus has found his true calling. Paul even jokes about this to Philemon, saying "formerly he was useless to you, but now he is indeed useful." There is a pun in the Greek—the name Onesimus' means "useful." In this passage, Paul uses the Greek synonym *euchrēstos*, meaning useful, and contrasts it with *achrēstos,* meaning useless. There is a further pun in that *achrēstos*, would sound like *achristos,* meaning "without Christ."

The style of the letter is light, almost playful, something the English translation can't quite convey. There is good reason for the light touch. Paul is going to ask Philemon for a favor, and not just any favor. He is going to ask Philemon to receive his slave back, not as a slave, but as a brother in Christ.

This will be difficult for Philemon, and Paul wouldn't ask him if he didn't think he was capable of doing it. But what an enormous pressure now on Philemon. To accede to Paul's request to take Onesimus back as a brother in Christ rather than as a slave would have created enormous resentment and jealousy among Philemon's other slaves. Is that what Paul intends? Perhaps Paul is hinting at manumission, where a slave buys out his owner and becomes a freedman, while continuing to work for his master. That's unlikely, as usually a slave would spend several years saving up to do so, and we know that Onesimus is a young man. Some people wonder why Paul doesn't condemn slavery in principle, but at the time slavery was thought of very differently than today. Slaves accounted for as much as a third of the population and were integral to the economy of the Roman Empire. They worked in building, mining and cleaning as well as in administration and commerce.

Paul helpfully offers to settle whatever debt Onesimus owes Philemon, despite Paul being broke and in prison. Paul is so impressed with his newest convert, and the work he has done for Paul, that he feels strongly that for Onesimus to return now to his former role as slave would be a huge mistake. His new life, initiated through baptism, marks a change not only in his own being but in his relations with others. That is what Paul is saying. We are all one in Christ, and Paul channels this by asking Philemon to welcome Onesimus as if he were welcoming Paul. The grace given to Philemon in his own conversion, he is now being called upon to exercise in charity towards Onesimus.

We sometimes think that God's love is given to us unconditionally, without expectation of any return, yet I can't help but see in this situation an expectation of a return for grace given. There is a cost to discipleship— for Philemon, initially it took the form of monetary support. Now Paul is making a new demand, by interposing between master and slave. He is seeking equality in Christ for Onesimus, and by doing so is highlighting the fact that discipleship sometimes means overturning the rules of normal, functioning society.

It's a shame we don't know the outcome, but we can surmise that the retaining of the letter points to a favorable response from Philemon, exemplifying his obedience to Paul, his trusting in God, and his possession of the essential Christian quality of humility. I also wonder if he came to see that the favor he was being asked to provide was actually a blessing in disguise, for him and for his church community.

There is a coda to this letter. It's a tantalizing fact that has come down the centuries which we very much want to be true, but cannot know for certain. It's this: that in AD 110, Ignatius, the Bishop of Antioch, was traveling to Rome where he would be martyred. Along the way, he was met by representatives of several churches who brought him food and drink and encouraged him in the faith. In return he gave them letters to take back to their churches. One of his visitors was someone called Onesimus, the bishop of Ephesus, of whom Ignatius speaks in glowing terms. Was this the same Onesimus, by this time 70 years old, who met Paul in prison all those years ago? If so, it would have been a remarkable testimony to the power of the new Christian movement to liberate and promote even former slaves to positions of authority and pastoral care.

In the end, however, we have to say we don't know. But it could explain why the letter to Philemon, so brief and so personal, was kept all that time, to eventually find its rightful place among the other writings of the New Testament.

With love and blessings,

Father David

Under Hamlet's Castle

October 10, 2019

William Shakespeare wrote the play Hamlet, Prince of Denmark, around the end of the sixteenth century. The play's central character is well known for his indecision and procrastination, which has fatal consequences for himself and almost everyone else. Even if you have never seen the play performed, you will probably be familiar with the speech which begins, "To be or not to be…"

It is unlikely Shakespeare ever visited the port city of Helsingør, (Elsinore), where the play is set. On the northern edge of the city, facing the sea, is Kronborg Castle, which has long claimed to be "Hamlet's" castle. These days it is a tourist attraction, which my wife and I visited during a vacation last week.

Upon entering the central courtyard of the castle, there are a number of doors into the castle rooms. We chose the first one, which led into the royal bedchambers of the King and Queen. They are depicted, one suspects, with the same imagination that fired Shakespeare when he was creating the character of the Danish prince. The furniture looked much more modern than the 13th century, when the real Hamlet is supposed to have lived. The four poster bed could have come from any century after AD 1600.

On the other side of the courtyard is a door marked "Castle Casements," which leads to the caves underneath the castle. We made our way inside, but it was so dark we struggled to see where we were; the few lanterns along the walls were barely sufficient to guide us over the cobbled floors. Walking through these darkened casements, I wondered about "health and safety"— what if I stumbled and broke my neck? The journey forward became a trial of concentration and trust.

However, after a while, stumbling around in the poorly lit dungeon of the castle stopped being a trial and became, in a perverse way, enjoyable. The inadequate lighting seemed to subvert the basic premise of making things easy for the tourist. Instead I became aware of the darkness, the faint light coming from a distant window, the sound of the sea outside. I imagined what it might have been like to live in this place—did they put the prisoners there? The thought was chilling. It was a relief finally to emerge into the central courtyard and into daylight.

A few days later my wife and I were in the well lit St. Albans Anglican Church in Copenhagen, listening to a sermon about faith. I recalled my experience stumbling in the dark at Kronborg Castle, and how it resembled, in some ways, the walk of faith. Having faith is an experience which often draws us into darkness. Once someone may have sold you Christianity as a tourist, telling you that faith is like turning on the light, and all you have to do to be saved is to "believe." But is that really true?

Faith opens to more than one definition. In chapter 11 of the letter to the Hebrews, faith is described as "the assurance of things hoped for, the conviction of things not seen." I would add that faith also involves trust (the walk in the dark) and revelation (faith as a gift from God). Everyone's faith journey is unique and particular: those without faith need to begin with prayer: "I believe; help my unbelief!" (Mark 9:24). Those with a weak faith may benefit from letting go of the need for certainty and enter a little into the darkness. Those whose faith is strong should regularly express their gratitude to God and enter fully into the servanthood which faith requires.

Resist the attempt to become a Christian Hamlet—"to believe or not to believe"—which is a kind of vanity. Not everything can be explained—if it could, then we wouldn't need faith! Instead, embrace the mystery of faith and don't be afraid of the darkness. Jesus was always warning his disciples about wanting proofs of faith. Like Hamlet, they were asking the wrong questions.

With joy and the blessings of faith,

Father David

The Unexpected Elevator

October 24, 2019

A funny thing happened last Saturday during the Celtic Eucharist. In the middle of the sermon, the elevator doors in the chapel opened and a person walked into the chapel (St. Barnabas has an elevator opening directly into its chapel).

The chapel service momentarily came to a halt, as everyone looked away from the lectern and towards the elevator. At first, our visitor looked surprised, as though she had walked into her neighbor's house by mistake. It was such a surreal moment that I imagined we were being filmed and that the recording would later appear on YouTube. Our guest began to lift chairs from the elevator into the side room. I then gently asked if she could put the chairs down and either join us or come back later, once the service was over.

Later I wondered how many chapels were there in the world which, along with the altar, lectern and religious art, also included an elevator? I asked myself, "is it possible that the elevator could be incorporated into our worship?" I began to imagine the elevator as the means of transporting souls. On the inside, there would be a single button showing the letter "H," representing Heaven or Hell. On entering the elevator, you press the button and hope for the best.

Would it work? I don't think so. God being God, if you pressed the button, the elevator probably wouldn't move at all. God is not a God of chance. But what about heaven and hell? Do we still believe there are two possible destinations in life?

I am reminded of the 12th century church of St. Botolph's, Hardham, West Sussex, where I served for three years. On the walls of the church are original paintings, now faded, which illustrate the choice between heaven and hell. In the original scheme, as you enter the church, you face either east or west. Facing east, you would see on the wall a scene from Revelation 4, with Christ on his throne surrounded by twenty-four elders, "dressed in white robes, with golden crowns on their heads." Facing west, at the other end of the church, the scene is very different: there, the devil is shoveling those condemned to eternal damnation into a cauldron of hot water.

It is a shocking yet impressive depiction of the outcome of choosing between the way of life (repentance) and the way of death (continuing in sin). Of course, few people in the twelfth century could read; the wall paintings were their gospel.

Although these days we tend to take a more nuanced approach to Christian life and faith, I cannot help but think that those Christians of the Middle Ages, who saw the choice between life and death so starkly, had a simpler and clearer vision of the way to salvation. It's a reminder to us of the Church's primary objective, which is to prepare our souls for the kingdom of heaven.

In a short space of time, my imagination has taken me from chapels to elevators to heaven, hell and salvation. But maybe that's not so different from those who saw heaven in a hazelnut (Julian of Norwich) or compared heaven to yeast in a loaf of bread (Jesus). Our imagination can take us in strange directions, and provide fresh insights.

The person who arrived in the chapel unexpectedly was in the right place, but perhaps at the wrong time. The chapel is the place where we meet God in word, prayer, sacrament and fellowship, and God may have been leading our visitor to the chapel intentionally. Of course, it may also have been a simple misunderstanding. Whenever I think of this story, I think of our visitor, so perhaps God wants me to do something about that.

With love and prayers,

Father David

A Walk in the Park

October 31, 2019

Even on a Saturday morning, there were hardly any people in Brandywine Creek State Park. It may have been the sign at the entrance, which read, "Archery Hunting is in Progress in the Park," that was keeping visitors away. I immediately thought of St. Sebastian, the patron saint of soldiers, who was martyred by archers—paintings of the saint typically show his body pierced with arrows.

Ignoring the warning, I made my way past the entrance and walked up the hill. It was a beautiful Fall morning. Along the path the fallen leaves had woven themselves into a patchwork of brown and yellow. If you didn't know the way, you wouldn't see the path, which may also have accounted for the

ARCHERY HUNTING IS IN PROGRESS IN THE PARK

OCTOBER 7 TO DECEMBER 14, 2019

IF YOU HAVE ANY QUESTIONS, PLEASE CALL THE OFFICE AT 302-577-3534

absence of fellow walkers. All of a sudden, I had the unpleasant sensation of cobwebs on my face; a spider that had spun its web overnight had now snared a prey too large to subdue and eat.

I continued past the large tree trunks which reached to the sky, unfolding their canopy of leaves at the top to catch the sun's rays. The trees themselves kept silent counsel, rooted to the ground where they grew.

As I moved through the park, I began to feel a deep sense of communion with my surroundings. I marveled at the beauty of the plants and trees and wildlife and how, occasionally, I would encounter another creature: a toad leaping to get out of my way, or a deer suddenly appearing a few feet away, or a woodpecker working on a rotted stump.

Every so often I would stop walking, and survey the terrain around me. It was in these moments of stillness that my soul felt uplifted, as I stood among the silent congregation of trees and thought of nothing, simply allowing myself to exist as a part of God's creation. I felt an unexpected sense of blessing in this place, and thanked God for the gift of the natural world in all of its beauty and mystery.

With peace and gratitude,

Father David

Re-Imagining the Crucifixion

November 6, 2019

O ne of the unfortunate consequences of the Reformation was the wholesale destruction of religious art. Throughout Europe in the sixteenth century, there was a wanton and systematic desecration of those aids to devotion which, over centuries past, had inspired so many of the faithful. Statues of saints were toppled or defaced, paintings were vandalized or burnt, and stained glass windows were smashed. In large churches and medieval cathedrals, walls that were covered in religious paintings were whitewashed to remove any evidence of religious art.

This destruction was ideologically driven: its purpose was to remove any trace of "idolatrous" imagery, and to stamp out the practice of seeking the prayers of saints in times of need. Instead, believers were to focus on the written word of the Bible, which became the sole authority in matters spiritual. The new religious landscape required undecorated churches without candles or any visual stimuli at all. Not even the sacrament of the Eucharist was safe; its celebration was relegated to once a month, or even once a year. As a consequence, altars shrank and pulpits grew, (as did the length of sermons). Thankfully, in the nineteenth century, the Protestant Church rediscovered the beauty of worship using our visual sense, and our religious practice is all the richer for it.

On a visit to Sweden last week I discovered, on the walls of the Krämarekapellet ("Tradesman's Chapel") in St. Peter's Church, Malmö, a striking example of what once was lost, but is now restored. They are frescoes from the fourteenth century, showing images of saints and representations from the life of Christ. That the paintings have survived at all is due to an incredible stroke of luck. Once the whole of St. Peter's Church would have been adorned with wall paintings, which during the Reformation were covered with whitewash. Then, in the mid nineteenth century, most of the church was knocked down as part of renovation work. However, the "Tradesman's Chapel" survived, only because the city fire department needed somewhere to store its equipment. The paintings were uncovered by chance during a 1904–1906 restoration.

Among the images saved is a painting of the crucifixion. It appears on the chapel wall at a height of twenty feet above ground level. It is a very different representation of the crucifixion to the ones we are used to seeing. Two angels unfurl what appears to be a large sheet or tapestry. On it, instead of a body on the cross, we get only the hands and feet, driven through with nails. We can identify a crown of thorns and in the center, the heart of Jesus—a real heart, with a clearly identifiable aorta. Then, as now, the heart is the center of emotional life; it is the core of the person and their center of being. In the gospel of John we read how "One of the soldiers pierced his side with a spear, and at once blood and water came out." *(19:34)*The artist shows the spear literally piercing Jesus' heart. The sense is clear: this is the work of man, to kill the Son of God and to break his heart, both truly and figuratively.

But the painting also reveals this to be the plan of God, because it is unrolled by the angels for our benefit. The pain and suffering of God—of Jesus on the Cross—is part of the saving plan of God for the world.

Even today, this idea is astounding—no rational human being could ever have devised such a plan. The crucifixion starkly exposes the profound beauty of God's love for us. I wondered if the medieval Christians felt the same mixture of guilt and exhilaration as I did, gazing at the image. I felt guilt for the evil that condemned and executed an innocent man, and exhilaration that God did not leave us in our sins, but saved us through the sacrifice of his only Son.

This may be an ancient story but it is still the same one which today speaks to our human condition. While our sins continue to pierce Jesus' heart, we are being saved continuously through his abundant, forgiving and healing love.

With joy and praise,

Father David

Becoming a US Citizen

November 21, 2019

T wo weeks ago, in the U.S. Courthouse in North King Street, Wilmington, I became a citizen of the United States. I was one of 61 new citizens, from 30 different countries, who had come to make the Pledge of Allegiance. Family and friends were also present, to give their support and watch the proceedings. At first, the mood in the courthouse was tense, as we were crammed together in one room, waiting for the judge to arrive. Unfortunately she was late, and after two hours had passed, those friends who had arrived on time had to return to work, before the ceremony was completed.

I should have guessed: if there's one thing I've learned in dealing with US immigration, it is that you need superhuman levels of patience. While waiting, I recalled the long and winding road that led me here: the endless forms, interviews, medical examinations, photographs, fingerprinting, and the sending off of checks at regular intervals.

In the courthouse, the mood of quiet tension gradually gave way to a party atmosphere. The judge finally arrived and spoke movingly about her own grandparents who were immigrants. The names of the new citizens were called, one by one, and each one in turn stepped forward to receive their Certificate of Naturalization. From the group of new citizens an Indian woman, a resident of over sixteen years, was invited to address the courtroom. She recalled something her father had told her before she traveled to the US. He said that she should be the "sweetness" in the mixture. Well, from 30 different countries, we were certainly a mixture.

Together we made the Pledge of Allegiance and now we were united under one flag. To cap the ceremony, a lady at the back of the courthouse sang the Star Spangled Banner. She didn't quite hit the top note, but it didn't matter. I felt an immense sense of relief that this journey was now over, and was overcome with emotion as family and friends congratulated me.

I wondered what this new status meant? Apart from the obvious one of being secure in my adopted homeland, I am conscious that there is now a new claim on my identity. I was a relatively late arrival as an immigrant. I fell in love with an American, and moved to the US from Great Britain at the end of 2015 and was married to Ruth in January 2016. It has been an extraordinary time since—it has felt, at times, like a dream living here, perhaps because it was unexpected, or because I have come to love the country and its people.

It is easy to make an analogy with religious ceremonies, like baptism and confirmation, which offer the gift of a new identity in Christ. In baptism Christians make the lavish claim that we are "reborn by the Holy Spirit." The oil of chrism is marked on the forehead with the sign of the cross as a seal of the Spirit. This ceremony, like the naturalization ceremony, is a public event. You are being re- ordered not only before God, but before a community of people who will affirm and support you in your new identity.

Although I now have a new identity to contend with, I realize that some things remain the same. Old habits die hard. When it comes to an early morning drink, I still prefer British tea over coffee. I miss bakeries that sell meat pies (although I found one in Savannah, Georgia). I like baseball, but for the sublime combination of tedium and excitement, nothing quite matches a five-day cricket test match.

If I had to choose the one identity which has had the greatest and most lasting impact, it would be my Christian identity. Whenever I compare myself to the person I was, say, thirty years ago, I know I am essentially the same person, but my identity has changed significantly. The Christian path through life has taken me in different and, at times, surprising directions, due to the benign influence of the Holy Spirit, the love of God the Father, and my love for Jesus.

I'll finish by sharing a special memory of my time here in the USA. It is Super Bowl Sunday, February 4, 2018, and the Philadelphia Eagles are in the finals. At the time, I was Rector of the Church of the Redeemer, Springfield, Pennsylvania. At the end of our celebration of the Holy Eucharist, I looked out at the congregation, decked in various shades of green, the Eagles' color. I picked out the man whose son sang the official version of the Philadelphia Eagles theme song, "Fly, Eagles, Fly," and asked him to lead us in singing the song. It was a rousing rendition—indeed, I doubt the congregation ever sang better.

Later that afternoon, my wife and I watched the Eagles win the Super Bowl. At the end of the game, the players and coach were interviewed by a TV reporter. One by one they gave thanks to Jesus Christ and paid tribute to the power of prayer. The football players were perfectly comfortable in their identity as Christians, and unafraid to give fulsome testimony to their faith.

After that, I added "Eagles fan" to my long list of identities. However, among my many identities, the most important identity remains that of "Christian." When life took an unexpected turn, and I arrived in the USA, it was my Christian faith that helped me to make sense of it all. For that I give heartfelt thanks to God, who continues to guide and bless me on this winding road. I am thankful too, for my American family and friends, and for the warm welcome you gave me when I arrived as a stranger on these shores.

With blessings,

Father David

God bless America!

Spaciousness

February 27, 2020

Earlier this month I read an essay by Cecile Andrews titled "The Spirituality of Everyday Life." In the essay she talks about the way we fill up the space in our lives with activity. She suggests asking yourself how often you find yourself with a free moment, and then reflexively reach for your cell phone, or move swiftly onto the next thing, without pausing to enter into a minute or two of silence and "presence?"

There are psychological reasons for avoiding empty spaces throughout the day. Freud noted our habit of repressing unpleasant thoughts and experiences, which bubble up from our subconscious if we give them room. But making space for them, Andrews argues, is precisely what we should be doing. "Space," she says, "is like sunlight and fresh air toward which the buried uglies of our souls crawl in search of healing."

She advocates giving time during the day to *being*. She discovers from her own experience that space, rather than being an empty void, is like a well of creativity and presence. Taking time each day, however long it may be, simply to *be*, can aid our self-understanding and make us aware of the presence of God. This practice moves us to the boundary of prayer, and for some it can be a way to enable God to bring things to mind. For others, the fear of what may arise from the subconscious will cause them to avoid doing anything to disturb the surface of their lives. Andrews identifies the area of resistance, "When people tell me they have trouble taking time for prayer or meditation, I often ask them what unpleasant things they might be wanting to avoid."

It was helpful for me to read her article during a retreat in Wernersville, Pennsylvania. When I first arrived at the retreat center, it took me a couple of days to adjust, because I was used to being busy and having my time occupied with activity. Here it was different: I was freed from my usual obligations and so was free to order each day as I liked. Soon I began to appreciate the sense of peace within and without, and how silence filled the space once occupied by noise and bustle.

Silence while on retreat offers a number of possibilities: there is space for reflection, for reading and, for me, the practice of Christian meditation. But away from prayer, books, meditation and distractions, one can simply sit and open up the mind to whatever may come. It is like stepping out from a crowded room into a vast expanse of wilderness. What will I encounter?

It is memory which makes the largest claim on my open and relaxed mind. The first things that came to mind painted a partial picture of a past event. Yet first impressions can be deceptive; the longer I rested, the more other aspects of the event seemed to fly in, creating a more rounded picture.

I am aware that memory can be unreliable, but on this occasion the practice of being still and open allowed a particular memory to be formed, which helped me to understand not only what was bad about it, but also what was good. Interestingly, it was the bad part of the memory which arrived first—if I hadn't made space for a longer period of time, then I would have walked away with a purely negative remembrance of a past event.

In the spaces which God gives us for receptive stillness, Andrews advises us to "seek the truth, not what is comfortable. Seek the real, not the easy." She advises setting aside some regular time each day, which at first may only be a few minutes. She writes that "a friend began each morning with only the time it took her coffee to percolate."

This practice is a good way of making space for God in your life. One of the insights from my own experience was to see how God was present at a particular time in my life, even though I wasn't aware of it then. Perhaps in the silence, God was generously sharing his own memory with me? I don't pretend to understand how it all works, but I am reassured by the knowledge that God is present throughout our lives and we are carried through by his unfailing love and care.

God's love be in your heart,

Father David

In Praise of Hermits

April 23, 2020

A s we remain in lockdown, I am missing the common social interactions I used to take for granted. I miss being able to visit people at home, especially when there is a pastoral need. I miss meeting people for lunch, or seeing them at church. Some of my need for social interaction is met via the telephone and internet—drinks at 5 pm over Zoom, anyone?—but living in our bunkers and communicating remotely doesn't have the same appeal as a genuine face to face encounter.

However, that's not the whole story. There is now more time for reading, reflection and prayer. I know that some people have enjoyed the enforced isolation and the freedom it has brought from the busy-ness of much of modern life. I wonder if God is using the current crisis to make people take their prayer life more seriously? It brings to mind a class of people the Church hardly ever mentions, but who have often been pivotal figures in the Church's history and growth.

These are the hermits. They are people who have willingly chosen to remove themselves from society in order to live a solitary life devoted to prayer. Christian hermits followed a tradition already established in Judaism and other religions, including Chinese Taoism (6th century BC) and Hinduism in the first century BC (the Upanishads). In our Christian story, the first hermit is John the Baptist, who famously lived as an ascetic in the deserts of Judea.

What spurs someone to leave society and seek the solitary life? A well known example is St. Anthony, the son of wealthy Christian parents, who left a life of material comfort to live a simple life as a hermit in the desert.

Anthony heard the words of Jesus, "If you wish to be perfect, go, sell your possessions, and give the money to the poor, and you will have treasure in heaven" (*Matthew 19:21*) and was prompted to radically change his life. He lived alone for twenty years in a deserted fort on the east bank of the Nile, about fifty miles south of Memphis, living on bread and water and fasting regularly. Eventually others followed his example and Anthony organized them into a loose community which would meet every Sunday for worship. These became known as the Desert Fathers, and St. Anthony is known as the father of Western monasticism.

The life of a hermit is, by necessity, one of spiritual discipline: of prayer and fasting, and of subduing the passions of anger, lust and jealousy which are inimical to a life of contemplation. When the soul is freed from worldly distractions and desires, there can be closer communion with God in body, mind and spirit.

Christian hermits share some common ground with members of other religions, such as the Islamic Sufi mystics, and indeed in the East the holy men and women are generally held in higher esteem than in our Western Church. We sometimes forget how important the monastic tradition has been to our Christian history, as a way of preserving our faith from the not always benign influence of the world. When Christian culture is compromised with its association with secular and political culture, as is often the case, a purer strain is often to be found in the world's remote monasteries and convents. At various points in its history, the Church has owed its survival and growth to the existence of these prayerful communities of men and women who glorify God by their humble lives of poverty, chastity and obedience.

There have been hermits in every age, including many impressive examples in the Eastern Orthodox church, including St. Sergius of Radonezh, St. Paraskeva Piatnitza, and St. Seraphim of Sarov. In the twentieth century, perhaps the most well-known hermit was the Trappist monk Thomas Merton, who wrote extensively about his calling and who struggled, not always successfully, to meet the demands of the solitary life.

The rewards of the hermit life are immeasurable, but to understand it you will need to experience it first hand yourself. Retreat centers and monasteries throughout the country offer an opportunity to experience hermit life and, with it, a taste of another way of being.

Hermits have left us with a treasury of wisdom, and so I will finish with some sayings of the Desert Fathers, to give a flavor of the hermit life. For a start, hermits cautioned against fleeing to the desert simply to escape other people: the monk Abbas Lucius once said, "If you haven't first conducted yourself well among men, you won't conduct yourself well in solitude."

The hermits extolled the virtue of silence: Abbas Diadochus said, "Just as if you leave open the door of the public baths the steam escapes and their virtue is lost, so the virtue of the person who talks a lot escapes the open door of the voice. This is why silence is a good thing; it's nothing less than the mother of wise thoughts."

The greatest spiritual sin is pride, which can unwittingly cause the fall of a righteous person. Isidorus the Preacher said, "If you practice your asceticism according to the rules, be careful, when you are fasting, not to get above yourself. If you find yourself feeling proud of your self-denial— eat meat immediately. It is far better to eat meat than to have inflated ideas about yourself."

Hermits who are steeped in prayer also tend to be practical. There is a story about St. John Colobos the Dwarf, who one day said to his brother, "I would like to be carefree like the angels who do not work but serve God unceasingly." And he threw off his cloak and went into the desert. A week later he came back to his brother and knocked at the door. "Who are you?" "I am John, your brother." "John has become an angel." He replied, "and no longer works with men." And though he cried out, his brother did not let him in until he had fretted outside all night. Then he opened the door saying, "You are a man and you must work to eat." John, having been taught discernment, made a bow saying: "Forgive me."

Have a blessed Eastertide,

Father David

The Church Yesterday and Today

May 4, 2020

W ith church services currently suspended, I have been thinking about the ways in which our church-going will be different when the lockdown is lifted. Will there be a different seating arrangement, or a restriction on the numbers of those attending, or different liturgical practices, e.g. a "no-touching" exchange of the Peace? Ultimately, it will be up to our diocese to decide, but in the meantime we can start thinking about what changes are needed to make worship welcoming and safe for all.

I am going to resist the temptation to speculate here on all the possibilities, but do bear in mind that when we gather again and we will gather again things will be different. Any changes need to address our basic need to gather and worship communally. While cyberspace has been our means of connection for the past two months, it doesn't properly replace what Christians have been doing for centuries meeting in one place to break bread and praise God.

It might be helpful to remember how it all started; how did Christians practice their faith in the early days of the Church? Last Sunday's reading from the Acts of the Apostles, written in the first century AD, provides a glimpse of what they did.

They devoted themselves to the apostles' teaching and fellowship, to the breaking of bread and the prayers…Day by day, as they spent much time together in the temple, they broke bread at home and ate their food with glad and generous hearts, praising God and having the goodwill of all the people. (Acts 2:42, 46, 47)

The Church's religious observance blended existing temple worship with the breaking of bread at home. The basic pattern was being set: of community, teaching, fellowship, prayer, worship and eucharist.

Less than a hundred years later, St. Justin Martyr (d. AD 165) wrote a description of a Christian gathering which will sound familiar to all of us. It is worth quoting at length:

On Sundays there is an assembly of all who live in towns or in the country, and the memoirs of the apostles or the writings of the prophets are read for as long as time allows. Then the reading is brought to an end, and the president delivers an address in which he admonishes and encourages us to imitate in our own lives the beautiful lessons we have heard read.

Then we all stand up together and pray. When we have finished the prayer, as I have said, bread and wine and water are brought up; the president offers prayers and thanksgiving as best he can, and the people say "Amen" as an expression of their agreement.

Then follows the distribution of the food over which the prayer of thanksgiving has been recited; all present receive some of it, and the deacons carry some to those who are absent. Those who are well provided for, if they wish to do so, contribute what each thinks fit; this is collected and left with the president, so that he can help the orphans and the widows and the sick, and all who are in need for any other reason, such as prisoners and visitors from abroad; in short he provides for all who are in want.

So on Sunday we all come together. This is the first day, on which God transformed darkness and matter and made the world; the day on which Jesus Christ our Savior rose from the dead. For on the day before Saturday he was crucified, and on the day after Saturday, that is the Sunday, he appeared to his apostles and disciples and taught them the truths which we have put before you for your consideration.

Justin is describing the practice of the Church of which we are members today. The Church has shown remarkable resilience in surviving throughout the centuries, having to contend with, among other things, plague, war, conquest, persecution, schism, reformation, counter-reformation, materialism, the worship of science and now, the coronavirus Covid-19.

When we look back at the early Church, we see the promotion and development of an ideal Christian *society*. If we turn again to the Acts of the Apostles, we read how:

> *All who believed were together and had all things in common; they would sell their possessions and goods and distribute the proceeds to all, as any had need. (Acts 2:44-45)*

This is the first Christian community, the living Church founded by Jesus whose mission was, in the words of Matthew's gospel, to "go, therefore, and make disciples of all the nations." In that it was successful, since we read that "day by day the Lord added to their number those who were being saved."

This is no fictional community, because Christians were observed and sometimes ridiculed by non-Christians. The Roman satirist Lucian pours scorn on the early Christians in a non-scriptural reference from the second century AD. He says:

> *...these misguided creatures start with the general conviction that they are immortal for all time, which explains their contempt of death and voluntary self-devotion which are so common among them...from the moment that they are converted, and deny the gods of Greece, and worship the crucified sage, and live after his laws. All this they take quite on faith, with the result that they despise all worldly goods alike, regarding them merely as common property.*

The idea of possessions held in common was not original to the Christian Church. The Greek philosopher Plato wrote approvingly in his dialogue *Critias*, of the early days of Athens, of a time when "none of its members possessed any private property, but they regarded all they had as the common property of all." The author Jamblicus, in his *Life of Pythagoras*, describes the sharing of possessions as the perfect fulfillment of the ideal of friendship.

We have come a long way since then, and I can't remember any time recently when our Church leaders encouraged Christians to hold all their possessions in common. It may strike us today as idealistic and naïve, but as an ideal it remains buried somewhere in the Church's DNA. It highlights a couple of basic ideas: that material possessions can't be transferred to the kingdom of heaven, and that if all wealth and possessions were shared around, no one would be in need.

What *has* continued to this day is the Church acting charitably to alleviate poverty. A Christian church is not meant to be a closed society, but one which looks out on the world. The Church embodies in its attitude and actions the message and life of Christ, who came "not to be served but to serve." (*Matthew 20:28*). Christians see in everyone the image of Christ, since "as you did it to one of the least of these... you did it to me." (*Matthew 25:40*)

Our roots lie in this early model of the Church, which we read about in the Acts of the Apostles and in the letters of the apostles. In these descriptions we find a spirit-led Church with charismatic figures like Peter and Paul bringing the word of God into the public squares and villages and towns around the Mediterranean. We see that, with God's grace, the world is waking up to the good news of Christ, to God's kingdom becoming a reality in the hearts and lives of his faithful people.

We should keep this history in mind when we come to work out the future path of the Church. Although we may feel that the coronavirus is disrupting our normal observance, which it is, it may be that God is speaking to us in our current situation about a renewal of the Church in a new and necessary way. Time will tell. In the meantime, the basic elements remain, which are to follow Jesus in loving God and neighbor, in building community and in meeting to break bread together. That last one we are without right now, but it will be central to our lives when we have the opportunity to gather once more.

May the Peace of Christ be with you all,

Father David

Rainbow in the Woods

May 7, 2020

W e had spent all morning and most of the afternoon indoors. Come the late afternoon, my wife and I were in need of a change of scene. We got in the car and drove to our favorite walking spot, the Brandywine Creek State Park. As we got out of the car, we looked up at the sky and noticed the darkening clouds. "Well," I observed, "if it rains, we have our raincoats, and after all, what difference will a little rain make?"

We were about ten minutes into the walk when the rain started to fall. At first a gentle sprinkling, which shortly after became heavier, followed by hailstones, small at first, but then like icy golfballs falling from heaven, a solid shower of them, so many that we felt under attack. Amidst the extraordinary noise of falling hailstones I shouted out something, but it went unheard. Our raincoats were taking most of the battering, and my trousers, shoes and socks were drenched. The heavenly assault didn't let up—it was ridiculous, almost comical, but what could we do?

I sheltered next to a tree, which helped a little. My wife went on ahead, but she didn't know I had stopped. Eventually the downpour eased up and then, as quickly as it had begun, it stopped altogether. My wife and I looked at each other and laughed. We were soaked to the skin. At that point, we decided that the best course of action was to make our way back to the car. And then we saw it.

A rainbow, unlike any I have seen before. This rainbow was not in the sky, but in the woods, nestling among the trees about twenty feet away. For a moment we were both transfixed, as we gazed at this vision, like something washed downed from heaven by the rain and hail. The top of the rainbow seemed only a few feet higher than our heads, and it held us in wonder. Then, as quickly as it had appeared, it went away, as though it had never been.

In one sense, the rainbow was a perfectly natural phenomenon. But the vision has stayed with me ever since.

Later it struck me that the rainbow in the woods was a kind of Easter motif, a symbol of the resurrected Jesus who suddenly appears and then disappears. The rainbow also speaks to our current situation, with the coronavirus having turned our lives upside down. We stay in our homes, waiting in uncertainty; or we go out, trying to avoid other people who may be carriers of the virus.

We are experiencing a national trauma, although at times, when I look out at the spring flowers and feel the sun on my face, I forget for a moment what has happened. And then I recall how different—how very different—life has become in such a short space of time. I don't really think it has sunk in yet.

The rainbow is a reminder of the presence of God who comes after the storm, who never really went away, and who welcomes us to share our fears and anxieties with him. It is a perpetual reminder to us not to lose hope or to despair, but to put into practice what we have learned. That God is present, and loving, and that through the power of the Holy Spirit he gives us strength to continue to live in Christ and to serve faithfully in the world. This short prayer seems to fit our current predicament.

> *God our comforter,*
> *send your Holy Spirit,*
> *to reveal your hidden mercy*
> *even in our failures and troubles;*
> *for the sake of Jesus Christ our Lord*

The following day someone asked me, "did you see the hailstorm yesterday?" I thought back to the experience of being in the woods during the hailstorm, and of being drenched from head to toe. While we were standing there in a daze from the heavy downpour, my wife and I were given a glimpse of something beautiful and mysterious.

The world is filled with miracles and wonders, and in our current time of trial, it is good to know that God is with us.

Father David

D H Lawrence
in New Mexico

July 23, 2020

How did D H Lawrence, the famous author of novels *Sons and Lovers* and *Women in Love*, come to live in a homesteader's cabin in the hills outside of Taos, New Mexico? In 1921 Lawrence and his wife Frieda had received an invitation from Mrs. Mabel Dodge Luhan, a wealthy New York socialite and arts patron, to establish an artists' colony in Taos. Lawrence accepted the invitation, and the couple left Europe for the USA, via Australia, before landing penniless at San Francisco. Graciously, Mrs. Luhan funded the last leg of the journey, and the Lawrences arrived at Taos in September 1922.

Their accommodation in the hills outside of Taos was primitive, to say the least, the cabins had dirt floors and Lawrence spent some time, with the help of three Pueblo Indians, repairing the buildings, adding new roofs and rebuilding the chimneys. At one point during the renovations, Lawrence covered his hand with a handkerchief and pushed the rats out from the chimney.

After spending a cold winter there, Frieda left for Europe, followed by Lawrence shortly after. Two years later they returned, this time accompanied by a friend, the artist Lady Dorothy Brett, who would type Lawrence's manuscripts in her small, monastic cabin, a stone's throw away from the Lawrences' own dwelling. Lawrence, who never stayed in one place too long, was to spend a total of eleven months in New Mexico. The couple left again in 1925, and Lawrence died in France in 1930. Frieda returned after Lawrence's death and made Taos her permanent home, as did Lady Brett.

On a visit to New Mexico earlier this month, my wife and I visited the Lawrence Ranch, as it is now called, and spent some time taking in the atmosphere of this beautiful place. We were the only visitors that day, and were welcomed by Ricardo, who now manages the ranch on behalf of the University of New Mexico. Ricardo's cat walked with us up the short path to the memorial where Lawrence is buried, and we stopped and took some pictures. Then we went to the homestead house and sat beside the. "Lawrence Tree," a beautiful pine, under which Lawrence would sit at a desk and write. The tree was later immortalized in a painting by Georgia O'Keefe. In the warm July sun, the place seemed like heaven on earth.

It may seem odd for a Christian priest to make a pilgrimage to the memorial of a pagan like Lawrence. He wrote in a time - the early twentieth century - when scientific, industrial, political and psychological developments were changing society and the way human beings understood themselves. While some benefitted from these changes, others became de-humanized by the forces of technology and the concurrent growth of communism and fascism. Lawrence resisted any "progress" which diminished the human soul. Lawrence wrote about the things closest to people's lives: the battleground of human relationships, the potential for change and transcendence, and he advocated for the unity of the natural world - ourselves included - to the cosmos.

The lack of visitors to the Lawrence Ranch may have been due to the coronavirus, but may also reflect the declining interest in Lawrence in recent years. How many people under the age of thirty have heard of him, I wonder? Nowadays, if you were to build an English curriculum, I doubt Lawrence would be included. Despite the strong female characters who populate his novels, he was a writer of his times, and a number of feminist writers since have expressed their disapproval of his work.

I read him when I was in my twenties and found his novels - especially *The Rainbow and Women in Love* - a revelation. From him I learned the importance of the wholeness of our human being mind, body, spirit and soul. Later I was able to make a connection between Lawrence and Psalm 139:13, which says, "I thank you, for I am fearfully and wonderfully made!"

What was the point of my pilgrimage? I think it was a way of reminding myself of a connection I had to someone, even someone whom I had never met. Lawrence was no saint, but he poured his life and the lives of others, not always flatteringly—into his art. In his own way he asserted the power of love - however messy and imperfect - to overcome the deadening influences of modern life. He remains a prophet for our age.

Blessings and peace,

Father David

St. Martha's

Bethany Beach

Petrified Forest

August 1, 2020

They say that age is only a number, but what if that number is 225 million years? That was the question I pondered as I stared at the petrified tree before me and tried to imagine it standing in some forest all those years ago.

Last month my wife and I spent a couple of weeks in New Mexico and Arizona. We had booked the vacation in January, and then Covid-19 came along, and we weren't sure if we were going to make it. But we did, and discovered one of the most beautiful areas of the United States. One of the benefits of taking vacation at this time is the absence of crowds; it was like taking a vacation in the 1950s.

The trip to the Petrified Forest in Arizona was a last minute one. It was my wife's idea and when she suggested it I said, "what's the point of going to see a lot of dead trees?" I didn't really know what to expect, but we had time on our hands and so we decided to make the visit. (By the way, when I paid our entrance fee I qualified as a "Senior"—a new category which I don't think I'm quite ready for.)

On a very hot day we drove into the park and discovered a vast desert area populated with random hills and mounds. The landscape was wide and alien, and it felt like we had landed on another planet. We drove slowly so as to take everything in. At the information center, the man behind the counter recommended we stop at the Blue Mesa, which was a few miles on. We drove up there and walked the mile or so around the strange, extra-terrestrial landscape.

Scattered among the terrain were the multi-colored petrified trees. Like fallen columns from an ancient temple, they lay haphazardly around the low hills. Close-up, the petrified trees were things of beauty. Years ago they fell into a river and were buried so quickly they avoided being broken down naturally. Now they existed as silent and mysterious witnesses to the passing of time. "Look at me," the tree seemed to be saying, "I have survived through 225 million years." It was as close as I've gotten to eternity.

Of course, the tree was dead—I was looking at a fossil, but I could see the bark and how big the tree was. No humans existed when the tree first grew. It existed without our needing to know it existed. We sometimes think we know everything, but the tree is a reminder that we don't. The tree was reminding me of my own limitations, at least where knowledge is concerned. I cannot know what environment the tree once inhabited. I can imagine it, but I cannot know it.

Likewise, as Christians we cannot know everything about the Palestine of Jesus's day, but through the Gospels and the other books of the Bible, we can imagine what it must have been like. Unlike the petrified trees, the words of the gospel are a living and breathing testament, and speak to us across the span of time. What God has revealed in Jesus Christ is eternally precious and valuable. Every generation must discover his story anew, and make it their own.

Jesus said, "Heaven and earth will pass away, but my words will not pass away." (*Matthew 24:35*) Jesus speaks to us a message that transcends time, but in time we must learn to discern the difference between what is eternal and what is passing away, and listen more carefully to the words of Jesus.

When it comes to matters of faith, there's no time to lose. I probably won't be around in 225 million years' time, despite the fact that I am now officially a "senior." Jesus said, "Follow me." He meant NOW.

With peace and blessings,

Father David

Wild God

August 15, 2020

My first week as Interim Rector at St. Martha's, Bethany Beach, coincided with the arrival of Hurricane Isaias. I remember being awakened early on Tuesday morning by a loud sequence of horn blasts which were emanating from my iphone; the accompanying message advised me to go to the basement. (I would have, if there was one). Soon after, Isaias arrived, sweeping through the town and leaving a trail of destruction in its wake.

By 9:30 am the rain had ceased, but the wind kept up. As I looked out from the window, I noticed two gates open, and went outside to make them secure. By now the wind was blowing fiercer than ever, bending the trees back and forth in a kind of wild tango. As I walked around the side of the house, I heard the sound of a large bough breaking away from the tree on the front lawn. It crashed down and completely covered the road, taking a piece of the corner fence with it. As I began to drag the broken bough off the road, a local resident suddenly appeared and offered to help—his appearance was timely, like an angel's, and the two of us were able to drag the bough off the road and onto the grass verge.

At that point the neighbor from across the road came out—we attempted a conversation, but the wind blew our words away. As if in anger, the wind then took my neighbor's glass door and flung it against the side, shattering the lower glass panel. At this point, without further attempts at conversation, we went inside to our respective houses and hunkered down.

Being outside in the storm was no doubt foolhardy and dangerous, but it was also exhilarating. It was a reminder of nature's untamed power, and of its destructiveness. A human being is effectively helpless in the face of nature unleashed.

The essential wildness of the created world, of which we are a part, is something that human beings have cleverly turned to their advantage. We build dams to create electricity from the flow of rivers. Once windmills were used to grind wheat; modern versions create energy. The partnership between nature and human ingenuity has brought many benefits, but occasionally the power of nature is too strong for us to harness or contain.

It's an apt metaphor for God, too, whom we sometimes attempt to "tame" and domesticate. We like to say that we know who God is, but any attempt to classify or define God offers only a limited picture. The wildness of God keeps him at arm's length, to some extent. In our search to know God, we reach an area in our understanding beyond which we can go no further, where we accept that, in some sense, God is beyond our comprehension. That's not to say that we can't draw close to God; on the contrary, those who have a deep relationship with God sometimes experience that wild power as a revelation of God's presence.

On the day of the storm, I reflected on the strange combination of exhilaration and helplessness I experienced when I went outside. It made me think of how God makes us alive while at the same time reminding us of his power to sweep everything away. God's power is both awe-inspiring and terrifying. To be alive in God! That, surely, is the purpose of our religion. You can study the Scriptures as a kind of academic discipline, but it won't make you alive. To be alive you have to step into God's wide world, and know the wild God whose power and strength is beyond our human understanding.

On your journey may you experience the wild and generous love of God!

Father David

Assateague Island

September 19, 2020

"Aztec Island?"

"No," my wife replied, "Assateague. There are wild horses there."

On a gray, drizzly Friday, we were discussing how to spend our day off. A visit to an unknown island sounded promising, especially one populated by wild horses. We checked the map: Assateague Island is located on a long barrier island which stretches like a strand of spun sugar from Ocean City, Maryland to Chincoteague, Virginia. In summer it's popular with campers, although from Bethany Beach you can drive there and back in a day, which is what we did.

Our route took us via Berlin, where by chance we stumbled upon St. Paul's Episcopal Church, a large, white painted, brick building. A parishioner happened to be leaving the building as we arrived, and she kindly unlocked the church and invited us in. The church has beautiful stained glass windows. As we walked towards the altar, I noticed the stale smell of incense. Last Sunday was their first time back since Covid, and twenty people had come. It was a beginning for them, as it is for us after this long time away. We thanked our host for showing us around and we continued on our journey.

We finally arrived at Assateague Island and drove across the bridge as, serendipitously, the radio played "Wild Horses" by the Rolling Stones. The actual wild horses were standing in a group by the side of the road, where a line of cars had pulled up. Human hands reached out to feed and stroke the horses, not far from the road sign forbidding human-horse fraternization. I guess people need that kind of thing, and the horses aren't

going to turn down an offer of food. We continued driving until continued driving until we reached Oceanside South Beach. That's as far as the road goes, unless you want to deflate the air in your tires and drive further along in the sand (for which you will need a special permit.)

We parked the car and got out. At the time it was raining, and the wind was blowing hard. We made our way across the sand to the water's edge, where the incoming tide covered our feet. A few gulls stood bracing themselves against the wind, and sandpipers darted in and out from the encroaching foam. As the waves rose and fell in the rough sea, we noticed there was no one swimming. In fact, there was hardly anyone there at all.

After a while the rain stopped, and we walked along the water's edge, leaving deep footprints in the sand. With the wind blowing and the sound

of waves crashing, it was easy to lose yourself in the present moment. After about a quarter of a mile, we turned back and retraced our earlier footsteps, whose impressions remained in the sand. It was like meeting yourself again moments earlier - like inhabiting two time zones at once.

Then, all of a sudden, the footprints ceased. The incoming tide had washed them away, leaving no trace. Normally, I wouldn't have thought twice about it, but instead I had the strange sensation of having disappeared. One minute I was walking and the next minute I wasn't. I felt as though I had been plucked out of the present moment and carried away to - where, exactly? It felt like a death experience, but one which came at the same moment as feeling very alive walking with my wife in that wild landscape.

It was humbling too, to think of having left no trace, although I knew that wasn't quite true - all of us are connected in some way or another and our influence, for good or bad, lives on after we die, in the lives of those we have touched.

If death teaches us anything, it is that life is a precious gift from God, and the best kind of life is one lived with God at its center. Our model for godly living is Jesus Christ, who regularly encountered death in his own life, whether in the demons which took possession of others, or in the attempts on his own life, or in the deaths of his friends such as John the Baptist and Lazarus. That's why Jesus spoke vividly about life, and the importance of living a good life, because death was never far away.

What does a godly life look like? Jesus summed it up in these two commandments: "You shall love the Lord your God with all your heart, and with all your soul, and with all your mind. This is the greatest and first commandment. And a second is like it: You shall love your neighbor as yourself." (Matthew 22:37- 39). Learning to live a godly life takes away the fear of death, and leads us into that divine life which is God's gift to us.

With peace and blessings,

Father David

Catch a Falling Leaf

November 14, 2020

"Catch a falling star and put it in your pocket,
Never let it fade away!"

Perry Como's song was a hit in 1957, and this week I found myself singing a variation of it as I walked along the leaf strewn paths of Brandywine Creek State Park. Fall is my favorite season, and looking up, I watched a flurry of leaves gradually descend to the forest floor below.

Have you ever tried to catch a leaf before it touches the ground? It isn't as easy as it looks. The harder you try, the more the leaf eludes your grasp. It turns out I was a better singer than leaf catcher, as each time I reached out for a falling leaf, it dodged my clumsy attempt at capture and sailed happily by. What was I doing wrong? The knack, I learned, is receive the falling leaf rather than to grab at it; open your hand and let it come to you.

It is the same with the receiving of God's blessings. The more you grasp at them, the less likely you are to obtain them. You can't expect to catch God's blessings every time, but you can make yourself receptive to them. God's blessings tend to fall on the humble and those without expectations, rather than on those who are looking to take something for themselves. Those qualities of humility and detachment lend themselves to the season of Advent, which traditionally is a season of penitence, (the other being Lent). It is a time of preparation, as we make ready to receive the greatest of all God's blessings—the birth of Jesus—at Christmas.

So when blessings come, be thankful and offer praise to God. If you miss out, then don't worry. God's blessings come in abundance, like leaves in the fall. Look to heaven and open your hands.

With every blessing,

Father David

In Memoriam
Three Guitarists

December 5, 2020

I will remember the year 2020, but not for the reasons you might think. It is the year of Covid, of course—although I share the sentiments of the person who recently complained: "I'm getting tired of being part of a major historical event."

But the other thing which will cause 2020 to be remembered, for me at least, is that this was the year when three of my favorite musicians died: João Gilberto, Julian Bream and Peter Green.

Well, as I was checking the dates, I discovered that João Gilberto actually died in 2019. But I want to include him in this meditation anyway, because the three musicians, each in their own musical genre, represent a high water mark in the expression of their art. They are all guitarists, which is a bias of mine - it's an instrument I have always loved.

Gilberto is the Brazilian guitarist who, along with the composer Antonio Carlos Jobim, actually invented a new musical genre: bossa nova. His most famous record was "The Girl from Ipanema," recorded with his then wife Astrud. Bossa nova enjoyed a brief heyday in the 1960s, and João was even invited by Jackie Kennedy to play at the White House.

As well as play guitar, Gilberto could sing (in Portuguese). His deep, sonorous voice, often sung in a whisper, complemented the harmonically complex and meditative guitar chords. He demanded a reverential quiet from his audience, and would stop playing to argue with a member of the audience who was making a noise, or even walk out of a concert halfway through if the microphones weren't right.

I had the good fortune to attend his sole UK concert, in London in 2000. I remember his concentration, which the audience returned—just a voice and a guitar on a large stage, and a respectful and attentive audience in awe at what it was hearing. At one point, during the song *Retrato Em Branco E Preto,* it seemed like we were being held in a different time and space. Concerts don't usually remind me of churchgoing, but this one did, for its transcendent and reverent quality.

Of the three musicians, the classical guitarist Julian Bream is perhaps the most well-known. I once saw him play a concert in a high school hall, in a large wood paneled room like an Oxford college. He came on stage wearing a dark suit, with a shiny black stripe down the side seam of his trousers. It was like seeing someone who had dressed for dinner in the 1950s. In one sense, the strictly formal dress was of a piece with the music, which was played with formality and precision. However, the  music affected me emotionally, and I was transported across the centuries on a kind of musical odyssey. Can music capture a particular feeling from a time past, I wondered? Would a 16th century person have felt these same emotions hearing this music as I did?

The third guitarist is Peter Green, who founded Fleetwood Mac in London in 1967. In the beginning, the band played mostly electric blues, but by the end of the '60s were playing folk, rock and free-form jazz/blues/rock. Green's playing was influenced by B. B. King, who was later to praise the Londoner as "the only one to give me the cold sweats." Green could play fast or slow and his timing, taste and musicianship were impeccable. Sometimes it's the notes you *don't* play which make a difference. Green taught me to listen for the spaces between the notes, as well as to the notes themselves. In his final Fleetwood Mac album, *Then Play On*, Green was singing about his personal relationship with God. His last recording with the band, the song *The Green Manalishi*, describes a nightmare encounter with the devil.

Green left the band he founded in 1970, and Fleetwood Mac later became one of the most successful bands in music history. Green's mental health declined after he left the group, and for a period in the 1970s he didn't play guitar at all. Eventually he made a comeback, but without the fire and ambition which had characterized the Mac years. I saw him play in London in 1981, and it was clear that his musical prowess had diminished. Yet he still had a rare gift for knowing the right note to play, without appearing flashy or trying to show off. With his blues background, he understood the importance of authenticity; in other words, he played with feeling. It was never his technique you first noticed, but the music itself.

So this year I say thank you and farewell to three musicians whom I never met personally, but who have long been a part of my life. Their music has given me joy, inspiration and peace. In them I discerned kindred souls speaking a language which I recognized and which has opened to me a pathway to hidden depths—to a reality beyond the reach of words.

With blessings,

Father David

Holy Enthusiasm

December 12, 2020

God sometimes nudges you in a particular direction—either in thought or action—by using a series of coincidences. Even the smallest ones can be significant. In morning Prayer last Thursday, I read these words, "Give us the strong faith of the apostles, and their fervor in preaching your word." They are similar to a prayer we are currently using in our Holy Eucharist Advent liturgy:

For the mission of the Church, that in faithful witness it may preach the Gospel to the ends of the earth, we pray to you, O Lord.

Then, in our Advent Study Course last week, our group was discussing the question of preaching the gospel—the good news—of Jesus Christ. How do you do that? One couple who attended the session related their own story of being asked by the Rector to go knocking on doors. I asked if they were prepared for this type of evangelizing? Not really, they replied, but they did it anyway. They discovered that, instead of being turned away, they found a welcome from the people they met, and an openness and willingness to hear the gospel message. God had already prepared the hearts of the people to receive the Word of God.

As Christians, we are called not only to believe in the gospel but to preach it. That doesn't mean knowing every chapter and verse of the Bible. It might be useful to quote a Bible verse now and again, in support of your argument, but do it too many times and people will start to feel dumb and unable to respond properly. In preaching the gospel, it is less our knowledge of the Bible that counts, than our willingness to share honestly our own experience of the faith, and how it has changed us.

To give a convincing witness of your faith, you will need to know:

1. Who Jesus is: the Son Of God and our Savior.
2. What Jesus did: he healed the sick, taught about the kingdom of heaven, and chose disciples to be the first leaders of the Christian church.
3. Why Jesus is important: he died for our sins and rose from the dead.
4. You also need to know that the reason was LOVE. "For God so loved the world that he gave his only Son, so that everyone who believes in him may not perish but may have eternal life." (*John 3:16*).

However, there is more to preaching than being able to talk about the gospel. The other thing you need is *enthusiasm*. It's a word which originally meant "god-inspired zeal." When preaching the gospel, your testimony will carry conviction and be more persuasive if you speak with enthusiasm, passion and zeal. Having what I call a "holy enthusiasm" gives space for your heart to speak, helps what you say to have a greater impact, and more effectively focuses attention on what is being said, so that it becomes less about you, and more about the message.

Like the people who received an unexpected knock on the door, there is a world that is waiting to hear the good news of Jesus Christ. St. Francis Xavier was a 16th century missionary who was filled with "god-inspired zeal". When he was in India, he wrote to St. Ignatius of Loyola, saying,

"Very many out here fail to become Christians simply because there is nobody available to make them Christians. I have very often had the notion to go round the universities of Europe, and especially Paris, and to shout aloud everywhere like a madman, and to bludgeon those people who have more learning than love, with these words: Alas, what an immense number of souls are excluded from heaven through your fault and thrust down to hell!"

It reminded me of my own zeal after ordination—I wanted to convert the whole world to Christianity. I knew it was an impossible task, but God put the notion into my head, and that idea—that possibility/impossibility —continues to motivate me to share the good news with as many people as possible.

By the way, if you aren't feeling very enthusiastic about preaching the gospel, then think of something you *are* enthusiastic about and then ask yourself, why not the gospel too? Which matters more? St. Francis Xavier reminds us that we are here not only for ourselves, but for others. What finer achievement in life is there than to save a lost soul, or provide a message of hope to someone in despair? Nothing! With the necessary enthusiasm, you have the power to do it. May God bless you with love, wisdom, and joy, and fill you with enthusiasm to spread the good news of Jesus Christ!

With the love of the Son and in the power of the Spirit,

Father David

Highway of Dreams

January 23, 2021

L ast weekend I dreamed I was driving along a highway in the middle of the ocean. As I maintained a steady speed, I stared at the unchanging road ahead of me and watched the highway disappear toward the horizon. Street lamps, left and right, counted themselves off. They had a hypnotic effect, like the ticking of a clock. For a while, time seemed to be of a different shape and proportion, as if it were being stretched out like the highway itself.

Above the horizon was a vast sky, shading to blue, with a sheet of white cloud partly drawn across it. The late afternoon light was muted, and the blue green sea lay beneath. As I drove along, my thoughts became loosed from their moorings and drifted off, like a seabird caught on the breeze. I felt a strange sense of peace, watching the road roll over the ocean and marveling at the strangeness of it all. This peace was like a kind of emptiness, without an object or thought at the center of it. My dream-like surroundings were having a soothing effect, and I entered happily into a state of other-worldliness.

As you may have guessed, my dream was in fact a reality, since I was describing what it was like to cross the Chesapeake Bay Bridge-Tunnel, a nearly eighteen mile long stretch of bridge and tunnel between Southeastern Virginia and the Delmarva Peninsula. My wife and I were returning from a couple of days break in Colonial Williamsburg, which also has a dream-like quality.

A combination of factors probably contributed to my experience: keeping to the same speed, the sense of movement, the absence of other traffic, being surrounded by water, and the length of the bridge-tunnel. But there was something else happening and it is hard for me to pin down exactly what it was. In religious terms, we like to say that the Spirit fills the world, but this was the opposite: it was a sense of not being filled, of emptiness, absence, but not in a way that felt wrong or problematic.

Perhaps it's easier to say that God is lurking in the empty spaces. Maybe. I remember a technique from the days when I practiced Christian meditation, which involved the repetition of a phrase or mantra for 25 minutes. The point was to train the mind to focus on a single small point. As you start to do it, you learn how difficult it is, and discover how the mind is like a monkey jumping from tree to tree. However, from time to time you enter a kind of stillness, which is really a blessed emptiness. This experience may be familiar to Buddhists, but Christians encounter it less often, perhaps because of our preference for a rational, practical Christianity.

There are many roads to understanding, and last Sunday I happened to find myself on one, both figuratively and literally. Later I reflected on the importance of being open to different experiences. Such experiences often come out of the blue, and they remind us that reality, or at least our perception of it, is less certain than we think. That's not necessarily a bad thing, if it is God's way of drawing us more closely into the mystery of his creation.

With every blessing on your journey,

Father David

Viewing the Corpse

February 13, 2021

The Benedictine monk Monsignor Augustine Hoey was a teacher, confessor and spiritual director in the Church of England and, later, the Roman Catholic Church. He worked well into his nineties, teaching and leading retreats in schools and churches. He died in 2017, a few months short of his 102nd birthday. A flavor of the character of the man is given in the obituary from the *Times of London*, which describes how…

> …*at the age of 98, Father Augustine Hoey felt in need of a 'fresh adventure'. So he left his old people's home in London to move to a tiny village in Norfolk. At Walsingham he cut a distinctive figure, walking at stately pace in his cassock and black soup-plate hat, clutching a Harrods bag containing his breviary. Long days of prayer, starting before 5am, occasionally ended with a tipple—he enjoyed champagne—in the local hostelry. An indefatigable 'fisher of souls', Hoey drew people like a magnet, whether aristocrats or beggars.*

Father Hoey was not above lending an occasional theatrical flourish to his lectures. Once, when addressing a congregation in church, he stood by an open coffin in the transept and invited the congregation to step forward. "Come and view the corpse," he intoned in his deep and mellifluous voice. Tentatively, the people stood up and made their way to the open coffin. As they looked in they saw, not the body of someone recently departed, but a mirror. The person they saw was themselves.

That's one way of being reminded of your mortality. Augustine Hoey had found a way to confront people with one of their deepest fears: the fear of death. Because death is a serious subject, he did this with a touch of black humor. He isn't the only person to approach death in this way. The

comedian Woody Allen once said, "I am not afraid of death, I just don't want to be there when it happens." Death, along with taxes, is one of life's certainties. Human beings were made for death, in the same way that we were made for life, love and laughter. At birth we receive a mortal body, and nothing we can do can stop the fact that we will grow old and eventually pass away.

Fear of death stems from fear of the unknown; what happens when we die? Those who have had near death experiences talk about going into a bright light. A parishioner I once knew, who "died" on the operating table, had an encounter with Jesus, who spoke to him. The parishioner revived to live a few more years. He always knew that he had been afforded a special privilege and, when the final curtain fell a few years later, he went at peace to meet his Lord again.

Not everyone, however, is lucky enough to have this kind of experience. For most of us, our understanding of life after death comes from the knowledge of the resurrection of Jesus Christ from the dead. It is Jesus who has overcome death and who now invites us to follow him into eternal life.

Indeed, his example and promise are all that we have; God, in his wisdom, has deemed that sufficient for us. Our confidence in the life after death, therefore, is a matter of faith. By the way, a fear of death is not necessarily a bad thing, if it quickens our faith. If nothing else, it should cause us to ponder our future. But when Augustine Hoey invited the congregation to "come and view the corpse," he didn't want to remind people of death, but of life. It was *life* that he meant to shock people into thinking about. If death is near, what does my life mean to me now?

That is a question for us to consider during Lent, which leads us to Good Friday and beyond. Lent may, on the surface, appear as a time of denial and mortification, but underneath it is really about the rebirth of the divine life within us. In Lent we repent of the sin which leads to death and we turn to Christ who brings us to life. This is why Lent is a preparation for baptism, when sins are cleansed and Christ claims us for his own.

Yet death is always near, and its proximity is not so much a shadow as a continual reminder of our need to choose life. We do that whenever we turn to Christ. The most effective power in helping us to turn away from death and towards life is love. The love we possess is a gift from God—indeed, it is his finest gift. In the Song of Songs, there are these lines: "Love is strong as death, passion fierce as the grave. Its flashes are flashes of fire, a raging flame." (*Song of Solomon 8:6*).

A love as strong and as passionate as the love of Christ seeks an answer in love: Christ's desire is for us to love him back. The love of Christ is real and can change your life. If you haven't already decided on your Lenten discipline, why not make it this? That, instead of giving up something, you offer yourself unconditionally and lovingly to God. The spiritual writer Father Gilbert Shaw once wrote, "The world has many lovers but God, alas, has few." Jesus was once asked which commandment in law was the greatest. He replied: "You shall love the Lord your God with all your heart, and with all your soul, and with all your mind." (*Matthew 22:37*) Love grows by loving, and love alone fully and completely answers love. Think about giving more love to God this year than you are used to giving.

Love can drive out our worst fears, including the fear of death. Those who peered inside the coffin and saw their face reflected, immediately smiled. One way of disarming death is to joke about it. The other way is to see how death is overcome by love, which is where we are headed on our Lenten journey.

With love and prayers,

Father David

A Lesson in Hospitality

February 27, 2021

The city of Oxford, England, is a popular destination for tourists, who come to admire its ancient stone buildings, narrow lanes and bookshops. Oxford is also well known for its university, which received a royal charter in the 13th century. The university comprises 38 colleges, one of which is Worcester College, which is where the Rector of my first church studied as preparation for ministry. Every year the college hosts an annual dinner for alumni, and one year he invited me to go with him.

We caught the train up from West Sussex and then walked the short distance from the train station to the college. Generally speaking, the colleges are like castles. Behind the college walls, students can study undisturbed within the ancient halls of academia. When we arrived at the side-door of the college, we showed our invitations and passed into the main quadrangle, from whence we made our way to the dining hall.

The hall was vast, and needed to be, to accommodate all the students. Rows of tables and chairs filled the hall. On the wood paneled walls hung large paintings of the deans of college past, stretching back centuries. At the end of the hall, on a raised platform, was the "top table": the place reserved for the dean and his dinner companions. We took our seats in the main body of the hall and waited. The dean and his guests were the last to arrive; he walked towards his place, stopped and asked for silence. He then said the grace for the whole assembly. We sat down to eat.

I noticed that the dean and his guests were the first to be served. His food arrived before ours. There was someone to fill his glass with wine and to attend to his needs throughout. When the meal was over, the dean and his guests were the first to leave.

This was an occasion rich in ceremony, formality and symbolism. We were observing how human behavior in the natural world can be ordered and codified. In this setting, the places of honor were reserved for the head of college and his guests. This was the way the college had functioned for hundreds of years, and would no doubt continue to do so in the years to come. Later, I compared our lunch to Jesus's instructions on hosting a lunch or dinner, as recorded in the gospel of Luke:

> When you give a luncheon or a dinner, do not invite your friends or your brothers or your relatives or rich neighbors, in case they may invite you in return, and you would be repaid. But when you give a banquet, invite the poor, the crippled, the lame, and the blind. And you will be blessed, because they cannot repay you, for you will be repaid at the resurrection of the righteous. (Luke 7:8–14)

The people with whom we sat at table that day were all graduates and most, I imagine, were enjoying successful careers. We were not at the type of banquet Jesus was describing. Where could you go to find a dinner like that? You would need to go to church, to experience the type of banquet Jesus had in mind. In the parable, Jesus is referring to a wedding banquet, which is what the Eucharist is like, where the Church—the bride—is united to the bridegroom, who is Christ. He feeds us with himself, and in the mystery of the sacrament unites us to God and one another.

Jesus is teaching about hospitality, where he seeks the company at dinner of "the poor, the crippled, the lame and the blind." For the meal is offered not merely for our stomachs, but for our healing. Who are these people he is referring to? We know them, or think we do, but maybe Jesus has someone else in mind. Could it be me, perhaps, to whom Jesus refers? If so, that begs the question, if Jesus calls the poor, in what way am I poor? Am I poor in charity, poor in compassion for my neighbor? And if Jesus calls the crippled, in what way am I crippled? Am I emotionally crippled with anger and resentment towards others? And if Jesus calls the blind, in what way am I blind? Do I fail to see Jesus among the poor and needy around me? Am I blind to the God who reaches out to me to heal my life?

Hospitality lies at the heart of the Bible message. When Jesus invites us to share a meal with him, he doesn't sit at the top table, but sits among us, as one of us. He dines with the righteous and with sinners alike. With Jesus, there is no "us" and "them," only "us." By the way, hospitality is a two way street. You can invite Jesus to your own banquet by making sure that no one is excluded from church. As soon as you place barriers to entry, whether by status, race or otherwise, it is no longer the church. Be willing to invite those who would not be expecting you to invite them, especially those who cannot pay you back.

I haven't been back to Worcester College since that day. It seems a long time ago now. The centuries-old ritual of having a meal together was so well practiced that it felt, at the time, like the most natural thing to do. In the gospel, Jesus provides us with a different and more challenging model of hospitality. In Jesus' vision, the church opens its doors and invites all comers to the banquet. It seems a riskier proposition, but the Church exists to fulfill Jesus' mission, not to reflect society at large. Where else can we receive God's grace, and be received as his guests?

With blessings,

Father David

Sermon Writing (with the help of Mani)

March 6, 2021

We own a cat, whose name is Mani. He used to belong to my step-daughter, but when she left for college, Mani stayed behind. He is the third "person" in our home. He has his own distinct personality, and enjoys the run of the "estate," including the Rectory and gardens.

He is eight years old and has gray and white coloring. At times he is like a dog, keeping guard. He will walk with us if we go out, only to separate

and then re-appear unexpectedly later. He is not a scaredy cat. I saw him once stare down a fox. Mani's tail was fluffed to twice its size, and he and the fox squared off at a distance of twenty feet, before the fox eventually backed down and slunk away.

Mani proves the old adage that, whereas dogs have owners, cats have staff. I sometimes think that our primary purpose in life is to feed him and give him the occasional treat, a.k.a. Party Time (those words we sometimes abbreviate to P.T.) He has set feeding times, at 7:00 am and 5:30 pm. However, on occasion—usually at 4:00 or 5:00 am—he will wake us up with an abject howl of distress, as though he had not been fed for a week. Although probably intended to elicit feelings of pity and guilt, the opposite is often the case, and the result is a succession of "go aways" from me and sometimes other words.

Occasionally he will bring us treats: a dead vole, several live birds and mice— even the lower half of a baby rabbit (ugh!). He is an adept hunter and a ruthless killer. He also likes to play with his prey, which we try to rescue and release when he isn't looking.

He is the cleanest cat I have ever known. His coat is immaculate and he takes great pride in his appearance. He hates being petted, and saves his affection— rubbing against our legs—for meal times. He sleeps alone in the guest room, which in his eyes is the main bedroom, whereas my wife and I sleep in the staff quarters.

There are times when he shows more affection, which is usually when I am working at my desk. Suddenly he will leap onto the desk and then proceed to walk on the computer keyboard. It happened last week, when I was writing the sermon for Sunday. Mani jumped onto the desk, and then curled up and went to sleep on my lap. He was purring away happily, when I realized that the only thing preventing him from falling onto the floor was my left arm. That meant I had only the use of my right hand to continue typing the sermon, which I did, one finger and one letter at a time.

Not surprisingly, this unusual situation had the effect of slowing down my thought processes. The sermon became more concise, and each word was carefully weighed before being typed. It was like a revelation, that here was a new way of writing, thanks to the cat curled up blissfully asleep on my lap.

At dinner time, I woke Mani up and the two of us headed for the kitchen, where I gave him some P.T. I had managed to finish off the sermon and it was a decent first draft. I usually say that writing sermons is a work of collaboration between the writer and the Holy Spirit, although on this occasion I am also prepared to give credit to Mani, our cat.

With every blessing,

Father David

for the Remembrance
of Him

April 10, 2021

Towards the end of his life, the Spanish filmmaker Luis Buñuel wrote an autobiography titled "My Last Gasp." (*Mon Dernier Soupir*). Buñuel belonged to the movement known as Surrealism, which included the painter Salvador Dali, with whom Buñuel made his first two films. Buñuel was raised by Jesuits, but in adulthood became an atheist. One of the charms of the book is its dry sense of humor: one chapter is entitled, "Still an Atheist, Thank God!"

Buñuel begins his autobiography with an account of visiting his mother, who in her later years suffered from memory loss. He recalls how he would walk into her room, then leave and walk in again; she would react as if she were seeing him for the first time. Eventually, she forgot his name. Reflecting on this experience, Buñuel writes:

"You have to begin to lose your memory, if only in bits and pieces, to realize that memory is what makes our lives. Life without memory is no life at all, just as an intelligence without the possibility of expression is not really an intelligence. Our memory is our coherence, our reason, our feeling, even our action. Without it, we are nothing."

The function of memory is central to the question of who we are and, as people of faith, why we worship. Why do we come to church? The answer is, in part, to develop a memory of ourselves as people of God. The particular memory that God fosters in us is one of *likeness*: we are born in God's image, and with reference to our divine character we begin, figuratively speaking, as an embryo. When we grow into adulthood, the choices we make will determine how far we achieve this true resemblance. How, then, do we grow into the full likeness of God?

One of the ways is to acquire a memory of our divine nature—the one into which we were born. As believers, our wider collective memory is recorded in the Bible, which gathers together stories about our past and our relationship to God. The Bible records a journey to freedom which began with Moses, who led the people out of slavery in Egypt. This journey continues through the obedience of Abraham and Sarah, the resourcefulness of Jacob, and the wisdom of Joseph. In the New Testament, we reach our destination in Jesus Christ, the one who is both radical and eternal. In Jesus, not only is a new life promised us, but a new memory.

Memory is not simply acquiring a history of what has been. Memory is a continual process of adding new experiences and encounters; for each person, memory is unique, however there are memories which are commonly held: the best example of the overlapping of a collective and individual memory is the Eucharist.

On Maundy Thursday last week, we heard the first recorded words of Jesus, from the first letter of Paul to the Corinthians. Jesus is in the upper room with the disciples, when he takes a loaf of bread, gives thanks, and then tells his companions, "This is my body that is for you. Do this in remembrance of me." Then, taking the cup of wine, he says, "This cup is the new covenant in my blood. Do this, as often as you drink it, in remembrance of me." Notice that Jesus explains the purpose of the command, which is that we do it in *remembrance* of him. Jesus wants us to remember him this way, in the sharing of bread and wine which he calls "my body and blood."

For this reason, the Eucharist creates a divine memory in us, which is why it has become the central act of Christian worship. The more often you attend worship, the deeper will this "memory" take root in you, and the more committed and informed your faith will become. We receive Jesus sacramentally in the consecrated bread and wine, which is our spiritual food. It prepares us to be "Christ" in the world—to speak and act on his behalf as his brothers and sisters, which means to love as he loves: generously and sometimes, sacrificially.

Luis Buñuel described our memory as "our coherence." A fully coherent memory is one which combines both the memory of our human life and the memory of our divine life. When Jesus commanded us to remember him in the Eucharist, he understood the importance of this ritual in building the divine memory within us. This is summed up in this instruction to the newly baptized in Jerusalem, from the fourth century AD.

> So let us partake with the fullest confidence that it is the body and blood of Christ. For his body has been bestowed on you under the figure of bread, and his blood under the figure of wine, so that by partaking of Christ's body and blood you may become one body and blood with him. This is how we become bearers of Christ, since his body and blood spreads throughout our limbs; this is how, in the blessed Peter's words, 'we become partakers of the divine nature'.

In the Eucharist, we remember the one who died and rose again. In the words of St. Paul, we are like those who are "dying, and see—we are alive" (*2 Corinthians 6:9*). Seen this way, worship becomes not just a chore or an obligation, but a way of being transformed into the likeness of Christ. Nourished by his body and blood at communion, God makes us alive in Christ, so that we may be his living memory in the world, and bless those waiting to hear God's story of salvation.

Father David

The Life Not Taken

April 17, 2021

H ave you ever imagined yourself living a different life to the one you have, or even being someone else? In his book, *On Not Being Someone Else,* Professor Andrew Miller ruminates on our "lives unled," the lives we would have lived if things had worked out differently. He asks himself, "what if I hadn't gone to a different college? What if my girlfriend hadn't broken up with me? What if my parents hadn't gotten a divorce? What if my wife and I hadn't had children?" Etc., etc. There are choices we make for ourselves, and which others make for us, that determine who we are and what our future will be.

Miller's *tour d'horizon* covers literature, psychology and movies. Miller cites Robert Frost's poem, "The Road Not Taken," as "a poem of metaphysical resignation, of sorrow at our inevitable relinquishments." The question left hanging at the end of the poem is, in what way would my life have been different if I had taken that other road? A mood of regret hovers over Miller's investigation: "There's loss to be found," he writes, "if you look, in the bare fact that you've had only one past and arrived at only one present."

The poet Philip Larkin diagnoses the problem in his ironic poem "To My Wife"

Matchless potential! But unlimited
Only so long as I elected nothing.

In Larkin's poem, the decision to do one thing closes the door to other possibilities. But is that in itself a bad thing? In electing to go one way, a myriad of new opportunities may emerge. Sometimes life is like a game of chess, where there can be many variations from a single move. Regret arises where the wrong choice is made; but then, like Frank Sinatra in "My Way," who has lived a life without regrets? It's a game you can play *ad infinitum:* to mull over what could have been. The main question is, where am I now, and does anything need to change?

Professor Miller doesn't include God in his survey, but from my own experience I can see the action of God in a number of pivotal moments in my own life. In these, I include both the good and the bad. God gives us free will, which includes thefreedom to make mistakes and end up in a bad place. However, the good news is that God does not abandon us to our fate; he is always reaching out to help us when the going gets tough. "God is our refuge and strength, a very present help in trouble." (Psalm 46:1)

When we place too much store in our own agency, it becomes easy to blame ourselves for not having the life we wanted. Generally speaking, we like to imagine ourselves faring better than we have already, and to underestimate the impact we have on others. In his book, Professor Miller analyses the movie "It's a Wonderful Life," starring James Stewart. The main character's frustration with his life leads him to contemplate suicide. It takes an angel to show him how the world would have looked without him. Much poorer, it turns out, and the revelation brings him to a greater self awareness. He discovers that he matters far more than he realizes.

Our faith teaches us that we are all made in the image of God, and each of us is a child loved by God. Our identity is unique, and each person has an inherent value in God's eyes. Wanting a life other than our own, or thinking it could have turned out better, is a fantasy. Learning to see ourselves as God sees us will build a picture of us that is more truthful, loving and forgiving, in contrast to the sometimes overly negative image we create for ourselves. Jesus said, "I came that they may have life, and have it abundantly." (*John 10:10*) Our invitation from Jesus is to receive this abundant life, which is greater than we realize, or even deserve, but which will help us to be the person God called us to be.

Easter blessings,

Father David

Spring Cannot Be Cancelled

May 1, 2021

I n November 2018, the painting, *Portrait of an Artist*, sold at auction in New York for $90 million. At the time, it was the highest sum paid for a work of art by a living artist. The artist in question, David Hockney, is alive and well at the age of 83, and his passion for creating art remains undimmed.

He is the subject of a recent book entitled, *Spring Cannot Be Cancelled*, which records Hockney in conversation with his friend, the art critic Martin Gayford. In 2019 Hockney moved to France, where he has a studio. He arrived in time to paint the arrival of spring; when Covid-19 began its grim march through the world, Hockney decided to stay put. The enforced isolation proved to be blessing, as the painter, working without distractions, applied himself to rendering in vibrant colors the surrounding Normandy countryside.

The book is partly a diary of that time, filled with pictures, musings and anecdotes. He remarked, "I'm sympathetic to anyone who's locked down on the twentieth floor. In a New York high-rise, it wouldn't be so good. But if you are in the right place, the lockdown has its pleasures. Here, it's just ravishing."

My acquaintance with the art of Hockney stretches back to the 1980s, when a friend of mine bought one of Hockney's Los Angeles pool paintings. Later, in 2012, I visited the Royal Academy in London, for the Hockney exhibition called *A Bigger Picture,* which lived up to its name, as it included the largest painting I have ever seen: *Bigger Trees Near Warter,* which measured 40 feet by 15 feet. Encountering this picture itself was astonishing, but even more so was the fact that the exhibition, which basically comprised pictures of trees, attracted the highest attendance for any exhibition that year.

At the time I wrote an enthusiastic "inspiration" for our church magazine, describing my own experience in viewing these paintings. (Sadly, the article wasn't published due to lack of space). With the passing of time, I have grown to admire the paintings more. Like Picasso in his old age, Hockney's current work has a child-like quality: the technique is simplified, the colors brighter. A child looks at the world with wonder, and sees things afresh every day. This child-like wonder explains, I think, why Hockney still has a passion to paint the world around him.

David Hockney, "The Entrance" 2019, Acrylic on 2 canvases
(91.4 x 121.9 cm each) 91.4 x 243.8 cm

A walk in the Brandywine Creek State Park last week inspired me with that same sense of wonder, as the late afternoon sun cut through the trees to light upon the rocks and trees beside the path. There is no greater artist than God, I said to myself, and praised God for his creation. Human art can render the same scene, albeit in a different way, which in itself is a cause for celebration. Hockney's art celebrates the natural world and at the same time makes new what is familiar: the hawthorn blossoms, the shades of cut grass, the contrasting color of a barn roof.

This meditation led me to think further on how art can open to us new ways of seeing God's glory around us, whether through our own eyes, or through the eye of the painter. In this world we have an honored place as God's creatures, who are endowed with the divine spark of the Creator. Like an artist, we can cultivate a vision which celebrates our world and each other. As each person is created and loved by God, our human relationships can be fashioned around God's artistic vision of love and unity.

That's not the same as seeing the world through rose-colored spectacles. It is rather about learning to see what is noble, good and true, even when these qualities appear to be lacking. It's the primary challenge for those who wish to obey Jesus' command to love God and to love our neighbor as ourselves.

We inhabit a world of connectedness, in a myriad of ways: of God to creation and of ourselves to God. Within this canvas, there are scenes of human interaction in which we are called to imitate the Creator—the supreme artist—in making and sustaining loving relationships.

Our vision is outward-looking, for we understand that appreciating and valuing the intrinsic worth of each human being is what makes us human. We are not the center of the world, and when we view the world this way, we are bound to be unhappy. A good artist is able to see both objectively and subjectively. They can depict life both from within and without, drawing lines of connectedness between God, themselves and others, in which new signs emerge to point the way forward.

In a Christian understanding, all signs point to Christ. The vastness of creation finds its particular meaning and purpose in the example of Jesus Christ, who showed a special love and care for each person. The deeper we are drawn through Christ into the beauty of creation—that is, into the work of the Creator—the clearer a true picture of the world, and of ourselves, emerges.

Therefore, through the artist's skill and vision, our lives are being fashioned into a new creation. The character of this new creation is spiritual—that is to say, it is of the essence of God—and its driving force is love. It expresses itself through a love for God and for neighbor. That is the picture God puts before us—are you ready to take your place in it?

With Easter blessings,

Father David

The Power of Love

May 8, 2021

O n a visit to New Jersey, my wife and I passed a billboard which read, "You can win this billboard." Unfortunately, by the time I started reading how, we had driven past. The words stuck, however, and I began to wonder what message I would want to share with the rest of the world (or at least with the drivers on the New Jersey Turnpike). The first slogan that came to mind was "GOD IS LOVE," but then I thought, wouldn't that exclude atheists? So I came up with an alternative: "LOVE IS REAL." It's not original—it comes from a John Lennon song called Love. In many ways, it doesn't seem appropriate for a billboard because the message is not trying to sell you anything. It is simply stating a fact.

"Love is real." What does that mean, exactly? Love is a small word with a hundred and one different meanings. Basically, love is what we need from the moment we are born, to the moment we die. Most of us learn about love from our mothers: as babies, we learn that love is nurturing, protective, and reciprocal. Later in life we learn how to express love as an adult, and we learn how the power of love can be both a wonderful and a terrible thing. We also learn of the love of God, which can teach us that love is much greater than we first thought.

Writers, poets and musicians have described and extolled love. The poet e.e. cummings wrote:

love is a place
& through this place of
love move
(with brightness of peace)
all places

A character in the novel, *Spring Fever*, by P. G. Wodehouse, said this about love:

> 'Love', she said, 'seems to pump me full of vitamins. It makes me feel as if the sun were shining and my hat was right and my shoes were right and my frock was right and my stockings were right, and somebody had just left me ten thousand a year.'

Bob Dylan, in his wistful song *I Threw It All Away*, reminds us of how love is precious, and easily lost through our own foolishness. In one of the lines, there is a perfect definition of love:

> Love is all there is, it makes the world go round, love and only love, it can't be denied.

Love is in our DNA, our very being. We exist because of love, and through love we become the person we were created to be. It's the reason God made heaven and earth. It's the reason God made you and me. For a

believer, it is God's love which fills the universe. It is a love which, as e.e. cummings writes, moves through all places.

Love's power can change lives: it can build up or break down. It can sustain individuals, families and churches, since true faith rests on a foundation of love. Love also has the power to wound and cause heartbreak. Whatever we think of love, it is true that love is flowing through the world like a mighty river, and there was a time when that great stream of love stood stock still and we were able to see into the very heart of it. That happened when God sent Jesus Christ into the world.

Presiding Bishop Michael Curry spoke about the love of Jesus in these words:

> Jesus sacrificed his life for the good of others, for the good of the other, for the well-being of the world, for us. That's what love is. Love is not selfish and self- centered. Love can be sacrificial, and in so doing, becomes redemptive. And that way of unselfish sacrificial redemptive love, changes lives and it can change this world.

Bishop Curry is talking about the love of God for us: a love which seeks not its own benefit, but the redemption of sinners. It is the love we see at the crucifixion of Jesus, which to human eyes appeared to be the defeat of love, but which in fact showed love at its most profound and far reaching. Love could never be more real than in the broken and battered body of our Lord Jesus Christ, who hung bleeding from the cross. Love could deliver no purer balm than the saving grace which flowed from the dying Jesus as he gave up his life for our sakes.

This is love in its purest and best form. It is the kind of love which surpasses all human expressions of love, although it comes from the same spring. The love shown on the cross henceforth becomes our reference point for love. So, for example, the power of love to heal is nothing less than the power of the cross to take away our sins. And the power of love to repair broken relationships is nothing less than the power of the cross to reconcile God and sinful humanity. And the power of love to forgive is the power of Jesus' words from the cross, when he says, "Forgive them Father, for they do not know what they are doing."

Through the cross, we enter deeply into the mystery and power of love to heal and transform the world. If we are to love and to be made in love, we need to remember the highest point of love which Jesus reached, which was on the cross. Whenever we gather in church to celebrate the Holy Eucharist, we remember Jesus' self-offering on the cross. The Eucharist is Love's memory.

"Love is real. Real is love." Take these words to heart and live in the power, and strength, and woundedness of love. Learn from the King of love, who is Jesus Christ our Lord. Let him teach you and inspire you and through him may you find love's joy and peace.

With Easter blessings,

Father David

Waiting for the Holy Spirit

May 13, 2021

At 6:00 am on a cloudless May morning, sixteen people stood on Bethany Beach and watched the sun rise. We had gathered to celebrate the Holy Eucharist of the Ascension of the Lord. As the sun emerged over the horizon, its rays spread across the beach like a heavenly benediction.

Standing on the sand, with the wind in our faces and the sun in our eyes, we were a church without walls, open to the elements and to public curiosity. A passing seagull might have looked down upon our small gathering and wondered what we were doing. We were a small congregation of Christians, drawn by love to stand and hear the words of Scripture and to receive the Holy Sacrament.

The Feast of the Ascension commemorates Jesus' return to his Father in heaven. From the disciples' point of view, the Ascension is like a second bereavement, following the Crucifixion. It is forty days since Easter, and they now occupy a liminal space—an in-between time—of waiting for the promised Holy Spirit. They were a small community: their number was around 120, according to the Acts of the Apostles: less in number, in fact, than St. Martha's today. What difference could this relatively tiny group of believers make?

As history shows, more than could be imagined. After Jesus's ascension, they returned to Jerusalem, where they "were constantly devoting themselves to prayer, together with certain women, including Mary the mother of Jesus, as well as his brothers." (*Acts 1:14*). While waiting for the Holy Spirit, they found strength and comfort in community and prayer. What else could they learn in this liminal space?

They are learning to trust the promises of Christ. They are turned inward, and discover that discipleship demands friendship as much as faith. Their introspection brings them face to face with the truth of their situation: as a small community of faith, they are without power. In this, they resemble their Lord Jesus, whose power came from a position of having no power at all. For the future success of their mission, the disciples will therefore be dependent on the presence of Holy Spirit.

There is a lesson here for the church: before we commit ourselves to any plan or task, or before we hoist our own flag, figuratively speaking, at St. Martha's, or before even we invite a friend or stranger into the church, we must first prepare the church for the incoming Spirit. Jesus founded the Church for this reason: first, to be a home for the Holy Spirit, and second, to be a door into heaven.

God blesses a church where the Holy Spirit has been invited. It enters those churches where people are turned to God in love and faith, and who are willing, like the disciples, to wait on God's word and be guided by the Holy Spirit. Our coming to church, our being together, our receiving the Eucharist, is our training for the work God is preparing for us. All of our actions and plans spring from this practice, which forms us into the body of Christ.

The early disciples looked up to heaven, but could see Jesus no longer. On the beach, in our church without ceiling or walls, we looked up and then down, and saw Jesus among us, in our love for one another and in our communion. We understood why he needed to ascend to be at the right hand of his Father in heaven. He can now be present to us at all times and in all places. It's a mystery, but a wonderful mystery.

Let your waiting be faithful. Love one another. Trust in God, who will not abandon you, but will come among you, and you will see wonders done in his name.

With Ascension day blessings

Father David

Taking Flight

Saturday, May 15, 2021

One of the best places to see birds in their natural habitat is the Bethany Beach Nature Center on Garfield Parkway. The Nature Center covers 26 acres of forested uplands, freshwater wetlands and tidal wetlands. It includes a nature trail and pier boardwalk which allows you to stroll through the wetlands without getting your feet wet. At the end of the boardwalk are a couple of benches, where I sometimes sit and watch the birdlife.

I'm not a regular bird watcher—called "twitchers" in the UK—but I enjoy observing them in the Nature Center, where there is usually something going on. One day last week, for example, I watched an osprey bring food to its young in one of the osprey nests. In the distance, two cranes flew from branch to branch, in a sort of clumsy *pas de deux*. A pine grosbeak, with its bright red vest, darted past. A white gull dive-bombed the river, over and over again, emerging and shaking its head like a cartoon character.

Seeing the birds swoop and soar made me wonder whether birds take pleasure in flying? They are only doing what they were born to do, and seem to enjoy being exactly how God intended them. It occurs to me that birds are often symbols of freedom, or strength. Our Holy Spirit is sometimes symbolized by a dove—a sign of peace. One of the national symbols of America is a bald eagle. In the Bible, God is compared to an eagle: "As an eagle stirs up its nest, and hovers over its young; as it spreads its wings, takes them up, and bears them aloft on its pinions, the Lord alone guided Jacob." (*Deut. 32:11*).

There's no sentimentality in the bird world; birds are, at the same time, graceful flyers and ruthless killers. When I lived in Coldwaltham, England, I once watched two crows deliberately and mercilessly peck a green woodpecker to death. By the time I ran out of the house, the woodpecker was beyond saving. It limped and hopped away from me as best it could, not knowing that I was trying to save it.

There's no doubt that human beings have been inspired by birds; we have even imitated them, by learning to fly, although we lack their grace and maneuverability. We speak favorably of having a "bird's eye view," but then make fun of someone by saying they have a "bird brain." They turn up in our proverbs and nursery rhymes, and if we want to know if a project will succeed, we ask, "does it have wings?"

Birds aren't domestic animals. They don't love you in the manner of a dog, and if you want a bird for a pet, you have to put it behind bars, like a criminal. It is possible to converse with a bird, which I have done a few times. There is a peculiar satisfaction in having a conversation in which neither party knows what the other is saying. However, if a bird is protecting its young, the conversation will not be amicable. One more thing: birds can sing! In Coldwaltham, I once went out at dusk for a walk and encountered a nightingale in full song: a true virtuoso of the bird world.

One of the reasons why birds are fascinating is that they have no need for human beings. The inspiration is entirely one way, which is humbling, because we think of ourselves as the most important creature on the planet. Birds, by and large, are indifferent to humans, except that they have learned to keep their distance from us, and with good reason: we are fond of trapping, killing and eating them.

It is said that St. Francis of Assisi, being inspired by the Holy Spirit, once preached to the birds, saying, "My sweet little sisters, birds of the sky, you are bound to heaven, to God, your Creator. In every beat of your wings and every note of your songs, praise him." The birds listened intently, and St. Francis blessed them.

Birds praise God by being true to their nature. But does the same principle apply to human beings? What does it mean for a human being to be true to their nature? In truth, we are blessed with natural gifts which we can use, either for good or evil. A natural human being who is raised without reference to God could reasonably think there is no greater being on earth than themselves. Human nature, left unchanged, has a strong tendency to seek power for itself, and this human drive can become both the means and the end of our existence.

Fortunately, human nature also possesses a divine element, which raises our nature to heaven even when we are grounded on earth. However, unless you are taught about it, this divine flame can burn, flicker and die. As modern education promotes more secular goals, I am reminded of what the Duke of Wellington once said: "Educate men without religion, and you make them but clever devils."

To realize our full human potential, our human nature requires an admixture of the divine nature, as revealed in the life and teaching of Jesus Christ. The fifth century bishop St. Cyril of Alexandria said that we should "put aside the natural way of life, and surrender once and for all to the laws of the Holy Spirit…so that he becomes woven into our being, and we are transformed, so to speak, into another nature."

With God, you are being oriented to a life filled with grace, where your natural gifts are placed in the service of your supernatural creator. A goal of our spiritual life is to surrender to God and assent to this new orientation.

As for birds, they are sometimes used as symbols of spiritual growth. I especially like the expression, "to spread your wings." The life of faith is like that: we spread our wings and learn to fly, becoming more confident as we apply ourselves to this new life. It's a special kind of freedom, rooted in faith, where we are borne aloft by the spirit of God.

As Christ ascends, so will we,

Father David

Translation Service

June 26, 2021

This week I stayed a few nights in a rented house in Selbyville, Delaware. The town has a very different vibe to Bethany Beach. It's a lot quieter, especially at this time of year. In the morning, more people are heading out to work, so I am guessing it has a smaller retirement age population. It also boasts a large number of Mexican restaurants.

I'm a relative newcomer to Mexican food. In the UK, the main immigrant restaurants are Indian. They tend to be family businesses, which means that they can keep the cost of labor down and provide a reasonably priced meal for the hungry. Indian cuisine is so well established in the UK that the most well known Indian dish in the world—Chicken Tikka Masala—is actually a British-Indian invention.

Last Monday evening I was hungry and ventured into Selbyville in search of food. I stopped at La Michoacana restaurant, on Church St., where outside is a small caravan selling drinks. Inside the caravan is a large statue of the Virgin Mary. The lady serving told me that this wasn't the restaurant, which was around the corner. When I entered, I lifted my eyes to the large menu board, which was entirely in Spanish.

I continued to the counter and looked across to where the food was being cooked. Flat bread filled with meat and cheese was slowly browning on the hot plate. Beside me a man waited patiently for his order, as I thought about what I wanted to eat. When at last the serving girl came up, I found there was a problem. As we exchanged blank stares, I realized she didn't speak a word of English, while I didn't speak a word of Spanish.

Fortunately, the man beside me at the counter offered to translate. My ignorance regarding Mexican food soon became apparent, but he patiently took me through the options, and eventually I placed my order. I can't exactly remember what it was I ordered, but it was something like home made pita bread stuffed with beef, with green sauce and a salad on the side. It was very tasty.

Afterwards it occurred to me that my experience on entering the restaurant was not unlike a person coming to church for the first time. Our church language, expressed in the liturgy, includes the Collect, the Gloria and the Creed. What would a newcomer make of it all? Without a patient translator, not very much. The role of "mediators" in church—by which I mean, baptized members who can explain what we do and why—is essential for putting newcomers at ease and teaching the articles of our faith.

The mediating role is a priestly one, and traditionally the priest is there to represent God to the people and the people to God. But our vocation as Christians requires everyone, at times, to assume this role, as "a royal priesthood, a holy nation, God's own people, in order that you may proclaim the mighty acts of him who called you out of darkness into his marvelous light." (*1 Peter 2:9*).

Through the helpful intervention of the man at the counter, I was guided in my desire to be fed, and likewise, we are to guide our brothers and sisters who have their own questions about the faith. Hence the importance of learning about the faith, and cultivating a prayer life, and attending church regularly. Our coming to church is not only about preparing us for the kingdom of God, but is equipping us to help those whom God has sent to us, to walk alongside us on the path of faith.

May your journey be blessed with many companions,

Father David

Amazing Grace

July 3, 2021

The words to the hymn, "Amazing Grace," were written by John Newton, a Church of England priest who was ordained in 1764. Long before ordination however, Newton saw service in the Royal Navy, where he gained a reputation for profanity and blasphemy. After deserting the Royal Navy, he found new work on board the slave ships coming out of Sierra Leone.

One night his ship was caught in a fierce storm off the coast of Ireland. The waves rose up and several crew members were washed overboard. Newton and a fellow sailor tied themselves to the ship's pump and worked for seven hours to keep the ship afloat. Newton then took the wheel, and for the next eleven hours steered the ship through the storm.

That was the beginning of Newton's conversion to Christianity. The man who once ridiculed believers and blasphemed against God, now pondered the future of his own soul. Could such a sinner ever be forgiven? The opening verse of "Amazing Grace," written in 1772, provides an answer,

Amazing grace! How sweet the sound
that saved a wretch like me!
I once was lost, but now am found,
was blind, but now I see.

Today, it is estimated that the hymn is sung around 10 million times each year. It was the closing song at a concert my wife and I attended last week at Ocean City Music Pier, New Jersey, featuring Judy Collins and Richard Thompson. Collins invited Thompson to join her on stage for the final number, with Thompson playing guitar. They began to sing "Amazing Grace," and then Collins called out to the audience to sing along.

It was a memorable finale to a wonderful concert. For me, this hymn has long has been a fellow traveler on my journey of faith. With simplicity and directness it conveys the generosity of God's grace, to pardon the sinner and rescue them from oblivion and death. It is a song of gratitude from the penitent who has turned back, and who now faces a life of hope instead of one of rancor and bitterness.

The hymn also awakens a sense of belonging. If we belong to God, how do we live secure under God's grace? The answer may best be found in John Newton's own experience during the storm, of being tied to the ship's pump. In doing so, he prevented himself from being swept overboard. If we belong to God, we bind ourselves to him by carrying the yoke of his law and accepting the moral claims of his religion. In return, God will protect and bless us. The alternative—a freedom to choose what you want on your own terms—is a dead end, as John Newton discovered. Only a life invested in God offers the hope of forgiveness and redemption.

Singing "Amazing Grace" in the concert hall was a different experience to singing it in church. At the gradual swell of sound from the audience rose, it became apparent that not everyone knew the words, or perhaps some felt awkward singing together. Judy Collins had introduced the song by describing it as the conversion song of a slave trader, and it is certainly true that John Newton in later life teamed up with the MP William Wilberforce to campaign against slavery. However, "Amazing Grace" is essentially a personal hymn about conversion and trust in God.

After the concert, it occurred to me that Judy Collins was following a time- honored practice among folk singers, of inviting the audience to sing along. As in church, it made one voice out of many. The power of "Amazing Grace" is to draw us in praise and thanksgiving to God. Sung together, or alone, or in a concert hall, it never fails to remind us of the eternal and amazing God, rich in mercy and abundant in grace.

May grace lead you home,

Father David

Gratitude

July 10, 2021

In his book, *No Man Is an Island,* the monk and spiritual writer Thomas Merton says: "If we are not grateful to God, we cannot taste the joy of finding him in creation…unless we are grateful for our own existence, we do not know who we are, and have not discovered what it really means to be and to live."

The Roman senator and orator Cicero described gratitude as "not only the greatest of virtues, but the parent of all others." All the great leaders and spiritual writers have emphasized the need for gratitude. St. Paul counsels us, that "whatever you do, in word or deed, do everything in the name of the Lord Jesus, giving thanks to God the Father through him." (*Colossians 3:17*) The capuchin monk Selanus Casey even recommends thanking God ahead of time, by saying "thank you" to God before each day begins.

When the Christian expresses gratitude, he or she is acknowledging the benevolent influence of God, and trusting in God's providence. To say "thank you" to God means to turn away from ourselves and towards God. This practice helps to cultivate an attitude of awareness of the loving and ineffable presence of God, not only in your life but in the life of the world around you.

Gratitude is the theme of our Sunday worship, especially when we celebrate the Holy Eucharist—itself a word which means "thanksgiving." In the Eucharist we are doing more than hearing God's word and praying together; we are receiving the sacrament of the body and blood of Christ.

This is a gift from God—and a command of Jesus to take it—which is a foretaste of heaven. The Eucharist unites us to Christ as one body and is one of the ways God literally feeds the faithful.

A church may experience joy, but without gratitude the joy is fleeting. Churches often fail or struggle to recruit or hold on to new members because gratitude is absent. A church without gratitude soon develops a corrosive culture of complaining, when you see everything that's wrong and nothing that's right. It's an old story. In the book of Exodus, "the whole congregation of the Israelites complained against Moses and Aaron in the wilderness." (16:2) People were going hungry and had become afraid they would die in the place where God had led them. God, however, continued to care for his people and fed them with quails and manna from heaven.

Perhaps the most difficult challenge for Christians is to be thankful in the face of loss, disappointment, or failure. Can we give thanks for all of those things? It would be understandable for someone to turn away from God at such times, or believe that somehow God does not really care. This is a test of our faith. What may make a difference is how well we are supported by our fellow Christians— our brothers and sisters in Christ who come to our side in times of suffering and loss.

If there is a blessing in adversity, it is that in thanksgiving we draw closer to one another and to God. In times of defeat or turmoil God is still loving us, blessing us, and binding up our wounds. In the prayer of General Thanksgiving it says, "we thank you also for those disappointments and failures that lead us to acknowledge our dependence on you alone." I would change the prayer to read "…our dependence on you and on the loving faithful."

We learn gratitude by practicing it, in our daily prayers and in all aspects of our common life. The supreme example of gratitude remains the Eucharist, and a beautiful description of it comes from the 18th century cleric Samuel Johnson, known as the "Father of the Episcopal Church in Connecticut," who wrote:

> …the Holy Sacrament is the most divine and heavenly Institution of our religion, and the most solemn act of our worship, the design of which is, to inspire our souls with a most grateful sense of the mighty love of our blessed lord and master in dying for us, in order to destroy both the power and guilt

of sin; and to seal a pardon to us upon our true repentance, and fill us with the most ardent devotion to God and our Lord Jesus, and the most affectionate charity one towards another...

When we receive Holy Communion, we are taught to reply to the words "The Body of Christ" with an "Amen." However, occasionally a communicant comes forward and replies, quite naturally, "thank you." Gratitude is our natural response to the gifts of God, and a soul which practices gratitude develops a lightness that allows them to ascend more easily in prayer to the God of love and kindness.

With a thankful heart,

Father David

All Things Must Pass

July 17, 2021

T he sermon was finished—the first draft, at any rate—and my head was spinning. In need of air and sunshine, I stepped outside on a hot July afternoon and walked to the garden behind the house, where the bees were pollinating the flowers and herbs. I stood watching them for a while, my head slowly emptying itself of thoughts.

The flowers were making the most of the sunshine. One of them looked like a miniature Christmas pudding, pierced with a hundred orange feathers and encircled with pink petals. The bees were flying to it. As I watched the bees at work, I felt a strange kinship with them; having spent most of the afternoon writing, I could now stop and admire my fellow workers. They reminded me of the bees in the vicarage garden at Coldwaltham, West Sussex, where I used to live.

The completion of a sermon usually brings with it a sense of satisfaction—of lightness, even—which lasts a few hours. In the enervating heat of the afternoon, this feeling of lightness intensified, and my mind began to wander. Remembering my former England home, I lost myself in a meditation on the impermanence of things. I remembered how the vicarage in Coldwaltham was hidden behind a large hedge, which shielded it from public view. It had large grounds that were full of strange, wild plants. I would often stroll among the grounds for inspiration, or when I needed a break from desk work. I loved the place, which was so large and impressive it drew a gasp of surprise from the bishop when he saw it.

After I left the property, it was empty for about a year, and then it was sold off. The hedge was cut back, which exposed the vicarage to the road traffic. The grounds were sold off too. The place as I knew it exists only in my memory.

There are other places I knew well, which are no longer. A house where I had once worked was demolished to make way for a road. A beloved church where I used to worship is now closed and turned into housing. They are reminders that things don't last forever. This melancholic reflection was interrupted by the realization that change doesn't always equal oblivion. I can recall places that haven't disappeared, but are still there, some of which are either improved or have been expanded. If there is a simple lesson, it is that change is inevitable, either for good or bad.

When you grow old, the past grows too and expands like a large field or wood, in which you can ramble. I resist the tug of nostalgia, because the present is always more interesting—or at least, it ought to be. Like artists or athletes who are always searching for the next challenge or mountain to climb, I try to look ahead, not behind. Having said that, in some ways a human being is nothing more than a collection of memories formed out of experiences, and an understanding of the past is essential for making right decisions about the future.

As for change, the evolutionists got it right when they said that a species needs to change and adapt in order to survive. However, the pace of change can be bewildering at times, especially in our modern age. Thank God then, for Jesus Christ, who "is the same yesterday and today and forever." *(Hebrews 13:8)*. While everything is passing away, God remains eternal and unchanging.

I could have spent longer in these thoughts, but my rumination in the languid heat was brought to an unexpected end by the appearance of a Christ Church sexton. We talked for a while and then he left me alone to enjoy the peace of the afternoon. By then, however, I had had enough of the sun and was ready to go back inside. I left the bees to their work, and made my way up to the house.

For all that has been, thanks be to God,

Father David

The Rectory

Christ Church Christiana Hundred

Wilmington

Learning to forgive

August 18, 2021

Learning to forgive is perhaps the most difficult demand of discipleship. When Jesus teaches his disciples how to pray, he places the words, "Forgive us our trespasses [sins], as we forgive those who trespass [sin] against us" at the center of his prayer. Forgiveness follows belief: if we begin by saying, "I believe," then we continue by saying "I forgive."

Forgive whom? "Those who sin against us"—in other words, those who have wronged us, harmed us or in any way denigrated us. Yet forgiveness of those who have sinned against us is not our first impulse. When we are wounded by another, we are more likely to respond in anger, and if we must forgive, then first we require an apology. No apology, no forgiveness. It makes sense, in a way, and if the world were fair, an apology would be forthcoming. But what do you do when there is no apology, or any acknowledgement of the hurt caused? The transgressor may have moved on, and you are left holding the toxic legacy of sin: a simmering resentment and a feeling of injustice. To remain like this will poison your soul, unless you take the initial steps towards forgiveness and healing your life.

To understand how to act, look carefully again at Jesus's words from the Lord's Prayer. They begin with a plea to God: "forgive us our sins." However sinned against we are, we too are sinners, and our relationships with others may well be complicated by our own sins, whether known or unknown. A question I often ask people when they tell me they don't sin, is "how do you know if you have sinned or not? Are you the best judge of yourself?" Refusing to admit your sins, including those of which you are unaware, is saying that you have no need of God's grace. It's a way of asserting your superiority over God.

If, on the other hand, you confess your sins, you are simply acknowledging your need for God's grace. God forgives, because without forgiveness, we would forever be defined by our wrongdoings and mistakes. God's forgiveness is an expression of his love for us, and allows the sin which impairs our relationship with God to be removed entirely. Forgiveness thereby draws us closer to God in gratitude and in love, and helps us to grow into the person God has called us to be.

There remains the difficulty, however, of following God's example by forgiving others. For this reason, in order to forgive we will often need to call on God to help us. Our prayer should therefore be, "Lord, help us to forgive others…" The poet Alexander Pope wrote: "To err is human, to forgive divine." Our forgiveness is both a human and a divine act: when we forgive, we imitate the divine power of God to forgive, yet do so from a position of human vulnerability and trust. We trust that this is the right thing to do, and that in forgiving, God will bless our act of forgiveness.

At this point I want to share a true life example of how forgiveness has the power to heal and transform human relationships. Several years ago a parishioner came to me asking to be married. There was only one problem: her parents had divorced many years before, and the marriage had ended in bitterness and animosity. In all the years since, there had been no forgiveness on either side. My parishioner was worried that the tensions between the two parents would erupt on the wedding day and spoil the wedding.

It was clear that the parents' lack of forgiveness had hurt not only themselves, but also those around them—the children especially, who had had to deal with their parents' breakup all their lives.

I sat down with her and we worked out a plan. The parents would be asked to meet the day before the wedding. It was to be made clear that the purpose of their meeting was to set aside their long held grievances, if not for their sakes, at least for the sake of the daughter who was getting married.

In the end the two parents agreed and the meeting took place. Miraculously, the old hurts and grievances melted away. Time had granted them both wisdom to see the wounds which they were carrying, and God's Spirit gave them compassion to let go of resentments which had entrapped them. It changed the family dynamic and allowed the wedding to proceed in an atmosphere of joy instead of tension.

God's will was done, which is another part of the Lord's Prayer: "thy will be done." That, and "forgive us our sins, as we forgive those who sin against us," are both connected. In learning to love, we must learn to forgive, for both love and forgiveness come from God.

Of course, it's easier said than done. A wise priest once told me that when you can't forgive, you should pray to God, "I want to forgive." And if that is too hard, to pray "I want to want to forgive." And if even that is too demanding, to pray "I want to want to want to forgive." And that's enough. God comes to your aid, and helps you with the process of forgiveness, especially when the wound is deep and you are feeling stuck. When we involve our lives with God, this is the sort of partnership he had in mind: difficult, messy, and demanding, but ultimately liberating, restorative and grace-filled.

With God's help, you can learn to forgive,

Father David

Interceding for Others

August 25, 2021

"Hello Father. Will you pray for me?" In Springfield, Pennsylvania, where I used to serve, that was a greeting I sometimes heard as I was walking along the street. Roman Catholics are taught to ask the priest to pray for them and, although I am an Episcopal priest and not a Roman Catholic one, I was always happy to oblige. I usually responded with a question of my own, which was "What is your name?" That helped me when, later on, I would recall the person and offer a prayer.

To pray for people and the needs of the world is called *intercession*. You are praying to God on behalf of someone else—you *intercede* for them. It's one of the things we do for one another and part of the work of building up the kingdom of God. Having a direct line to God is a freedom that needs to be exercised as often as possible! When you pray for someone you are plugging into a network of love which connects you to the person and to God at the same time.

The Book of Common Prayer has a section called "Prayers of the People," which includes prayers for ourselves and for others. There is an order to the prayer, usually beginning with the Church, bishops and other Church leaders, the Church's mission and the world, the President and Governor, the church community, the sick and needy, and finally there are prayers for the departed. Sometimes there is space to add extra prayers; silence is another option. Prayers need time, and that is one of the demands prayer makes of us.

Prayer makes other demands too. To pray is to remember—a face, an event, an intractable problem. We bring the past to bear in our present situation, in order to influence a future outcome. Prayer works in and around time in a mysterious way, but the main thing is simply to pray. Painful memories are easier to bear when you pray—prayer is an avenue of healing.

It's important to get the intention right when you pray. Although prayer springs from love, a loving prayer may not always be the right one. I know of someone who had a partner who was nearing the end of his life, one that was filled with pain. Out of a loving intention, the person asked God to end the life of her loved one. Although the prayer was well meant, it was wrong to pray for another person's death. In this case, a prayer for mercy would have been preferable.

When you pray to God, you recall the words of Jesus, who taught "thy will be done." Underpinning our understanding about prayer is that God has the final say. Prayer doesn't always get you the result you want, which makes some people doubt that prayer works. In prayer we submit to God's will, trusting in him to answer our prayer in the way that will be to the benefit of ourselves and for those for whom we pray. The fact is, we don't always know what is best for us, but God does, (thank God!) which is why the answer to prayer can surprise us. God can be relied on, whenever we pray in faith.

Jesus once remarked that his Father in heaven hid spiritual truths "from the wise and the intelligent and revealed them to infants." (*Matthew 11:25*). I know from my own experience that you can learn much about how to pray by observing children at prayer. The first thing you discover is that prayer comes naturally to them. It seems that prayer is an inbuilt part of our human nature. To pray is to be human. The other thing you notice, when children pray, is their trust in God. As they are used to living under authority, they have fewer problems accepting God as a supreme authority.

Years ago I was in charge of our church's Sunday School, and every Sunday the children and I would begin with prayer. I set up a prayer station or mini-shrine, with candles and a picture of Jesus. We would light the candles and get down on our knees. I would invite the children to pray, and they would call out names that came to mind—not always people, as it turned out: pets were regularly included, including some pet rats. On one occasion, one of the boys prayed for his favorite football team, Manchester United. Later in the prayer he asked God to make sure the other team lost the match that afternoon. At that point I interrupted the prayer to remind the children that prayer is a power for good in the world, and our intercessions are not intended for the destruction or harm of those for whom we pray. (If I recall rightly, the football match ended in a tie).

To be a good intercessor, you need to be a good listener. You are to be alert to people and situations, and their need for someone to pray for them. Your intercessions for others can be specific: prayers at a hospital bedside, for example, when you ask for healing, can help both the patient and the petitioner. At other times, you can pray for more general situations, such as an end to war, or for the healing of societal divisions. Your prayer can be as brief or as long as is necessary. At times you can sit in silence before God, while being open to the Spirit's promptings. Intercession should have a structure which provides the freedom to pray for whatever comes to mind. Pray as you can, not as you can't.

The prayer of intercession is the heartbeat of any church—when its prayer is strong, the church is healthy, even if there is a small congregation. For those of you who intercede already, may God bless you and continue to strengthen your prayer. If you are a novice at prayer, then follow Jesus' advice—it is very simple: "whenever you pray, go into your room and shut the door and pray to your Father who is in secret; and your Father who sees in secret will reward you." (*Matthew 6:6*) Amen to that!

With every blessing,

Father David

About the Author

    David Beresford trained for the Anglican priesthood at the College of the Resurrection, Mirfield, West Yorkshire, where he was awarded a First in Theology and Pastoral Studies in 2009. He received a post- graduate diploma in Ministry and Mission from the University of Sussex in 2012 and trained as a Spiritual Director for the Diocese of Chichester, England in 2013. He has created and led a number of study courses, including *Faith and Poetry, Learning to Pray, God and Us* and *Art and Faith.* He also leads retreats and Quiet Days. He has served in parishes in West Sussex and Bedfordshire, England, including prison chaplaincy, as well as in Pennsylvania and Delaware, USA. He currently lives in Wilmington, Delaware, with his wife Ruth, who is also a priest.

— Colophon —

Above & Below, Reflections on the Spiritual Journey was designed in Italy by Bob Schwartz on an Apple MacPro using Adobe InDesign and Photoshop CC. The book title and the chapter titles were set in eighty-seven point and fourty-eight-point Meditation, respectively. Primary text was set in twelve-point Perpetua, fourteen-point leaded. The front and back material text was set in ten-point Poppins, thirteen- point leaded. Poppins was also used in various weights for the book's sub-title, main-chapter sub-titles, running footers and front and back material titles.

Meditation is a "smooth and peaceful" sans serif font, designed in 2014 by French typographer, Florian Bambhout of Bambootypes.

Perpetua—designed by English sculptor and stonemason Eric Gill for the British Monotype Corporation—is a transitional serif typeface that was commissioned at the request of Stanley Morison, an influential historian of printing and adviser to Monotype around 1925 and was named for the Christian martyr Vibia Perpetua.

Poppins is a geometric sans-serif typeface published by Indian Type Foundry in 2014. Indian Type Foundry describes Poppins as "an internationalist take on the geometric sans genre."

www.ingramcontent.com/pod-product-compliance
Lightning Source LLC
Chambersburg PA
CBHW051316120626
46547CB00015B/2260